Londejny Super 2005

THE POLEMICS OF IMAGINATION

The POLEMICS of IMAGINATION

*Selected Essays on Art
Culture and Society*

PETER ABBS

SKOOB BOOKS PUBLISHING
LONDON

Published in 1996 by
SKOOB BOOKS LTD
11a-17 Sicilian Avenue
Southampton Row
Holborn
London WC1A 2QH

First edition

Series editor: Christopher Johnson
Design © Mark Lovell

ISBN 1 871438 31 4

Printed by WSOY, Finland

British Library Cataloguing-in-Publication Data
A catalogue record for this book is available
from the British Library.

CONTENTS

Poetry

For Man and Islands
Songs of a New Taliesin
Icons of Time
Personae and Other Selected Poems

On the Theory of English Teaching

English for Diversity
Root and Blossom: the Philosophy, Practice
and Politics of English Teaching
English Within the Arts

Practical Guides to the Forms of Literature

The Forms of Poetry
The Forms of Narrative

On Culture, the Arts and Education

Autobiography in Education: An Introduction to
the Subjective Discipline of Autobiography
and its central place in the Education of Teachers
Proposal for a New College (with Graham Carey)
Reclamations: Essays on Culture, Mass-Culture and the Curriculum
A is for Aesthetic: Essays on Creative and Aesthetic Education
The Educational Imperative: In Defence of Socratic
and Aesthetic Learning.

Edited Symposia on the Arts

The Black Rainbow: Essays on the Present Breakdown of Culture
Living Powers: The Arts in Education
The Symbolic Order: a Contemporary Reader on the Arts Debate

Author's Note

The main aim of *The Polemics of Imagination* is to argue for the poetic, the aesthetic and the spiritual; and the need for their profound recognition in our fast unravelling civilisation.

The volume divides into four parts. The first section examines critically both Modernism and Post Modernism. The second section offers a defence of aesthetic education as one part of the question as how to meet creatively the current insensibility and general social dissolution. The arts matter because, at their best, they educate, extend and refine the life of feeling and open up ways of understanding through the agency of the imagination. The third section looks at the art of autobiography through a similar lens. In the act of autobiography the intimate and the personally confused can be brought into the common realm to seek their verification and acceptance. Here we find a genre which is committed to the movement from the dark recesses of memory into the light of common day. For what compels the autobiographer but a desire for wholeness, and the integration of contending claims and differences? Finally, the collection of essays ends on poetry. It offers an analysis of the present plight of poetry - one of our greatest art forms and the one closest to extinction - and argues for a more ambitious form of poetry with its roots in myth, archetype and history.

The essays gathered here have been written at different times and for different contexts. The earliest was published in 1979, the latest in the Autumn of 1993. I have resisted the urge to revise extensively, though I have deleted some repetitive material. Readers may detect some shifts in my thinking. I hope so; but I also hope they may sense an underlying logic and a consistent commitment to the primacy of the aesthetic response and the power of the imagination.

Finally, I must thank Pat Bone, my secretary, for all the labour she has put into this project. I am indebted to her support and patience. Quite simply, without her there would be no book.

Peter Abbs
University of Sussex
Spring 1994

We have to believe in a God who is
like the true God in everything
except that he does not exist, for
we have not yet reached the point
where God exists

SIMONE WEIL

INTRODUCTION

Peter Abbs' collection of essays ought to be required reading for everyone engaged in education, from nursery school to university and beyond. Abbs' main contention is that the arts are an essential part of education, and that 'the aesthetic refers to a basic modality of human intelligence'. Yet the politicians responsible for educational policy in this country are eager to cut costs by treating the arts as 'extras'. The political culture of our time, overshadowed as it was for too many years by the philistine Margaret Thatcher, perceives education merely as a way of ensuring that pupils can find gainful employment, whereas it should be concerned with promoting the intellectual and emotional development of the whole individual. In that development, the arts play a vital part.

In Abbs' view, 'we have failed to develop any adequate public conception of the true significance of the arts'. I am certain that he is right in regarding the aesthetic as a basic modality of human intelligence. As the Harvard psychologist Howard Gardner pointed out, human intelligence is multiple rather than single. The scientific revolution has inclined us to value above all other varieties, the kind of detached, abstract intelligence required by physicists, mathematicians, and philosophers, which sharply separates the subjective from the objective. But aesthetic intelligence, which enables us to comprehend and order our feelings, is equally important. Mozart, perhaps the most gifted composer who ever lived, is just as *intelligent* as Newton, but in an entirely different fashion. Nietzsche perceived music as so significant that it made life worth living. In his view, 'It is only as *an aesthetic phenomenon* that existence and the world are eternally *justified*'. The arts reintegrate intellect and emotion, mind and body; and those who, because of lack of opportunity, have had no education in, or exposure to, the arts, are crippled human beings.

This could not happen in pre-literate cultures in which music, dancing, painting, sculpture and pottery are an integral part of collective living. In such cultures, the arts are for everyone, not the preserve of a precious few. In Abbs' view, Modernism has a lot to answer for. By attempting to make a clean break with past aesthetic traditions, many artists, however innovative, ran into blind alleys which led nowhere. Aesthetic judgement became corrupted by fashion. A work was only considered valuable if it was perceived as individual, advanced, and preferably shocking. Abbs is surely right in insisting that artistic innovation, the life-blood of the arts, must nevertheless be based upon a knowledge and appreciation of what has gone before. A scientist need not read Newton's original papers, for Newton's discoveries have been incorporated into the scientific edifice, and his picture of the universe has been superseded. Modernism tended to assume that the same kind of historical progress applied to the arts. But the arts are different. Beethoven and Rembrandt can never be superseded. Abbs believes that art teachers can foster creativity whilst also teaching appreciation of our cultural heritage. As he puts it succinctly: 'As art teachers it is our task to create both *careful readers and piratical raiders*'.

One art of which Abbs has made a special study is that of auto-biography, which he believes to be a genre of literature relatively neglected by literary critics. Many autobiographies, like those of politicians and film-stars, are no more than narcissistic chronicles of conventional success. But others, like Gosse's *Father and Son,* are attempts at self-discovery; efforts toward individuation. 'Autobiography may provide us with the lost key to the door of our own existence and a way forward - if the door opens and if we have the courage to go on'. Abbs uses autobiography in teaching. In the belief that knowledge, if it is to be of any real value, must become a part of the student's life, not just an intellectual acquisition, Abbs encourages his students to render some autobiographical account of their own lives and share it with their fellows. The results are often surprising. When an anxious, insecure student brings to a class something of him or herself, a new confidence is engendered which makes learning more personally related, less formidable, and therefore easier.

Abbs' own autobiography is of particular interest. He comes from the rural working class, and his anger at the lack of any cultural dimension in his education is one powerful motive force informing his own teaching. During thirteen years of Catholic education he became expert in many aspects of Catholic theology but 'I did not once paint a picture, write a poem, pick up a musical instrument, make ceramics or sculpture, do dramatic improvisation or any mime or dance ... . At sixteen, I had simply not heard of Mozart or Beethoven, of Leonardo da Vinci or Picasso'. Like many of the best educated people, Abbs is largely self-educated. His passion for reading began in adolescence, when books, absent from his home but available in second-hand bookshops, became a magic key to understanding.

Abbs is not only a teacher and a critic, but also a poet. His last three chapters are concerned with the failure of modern poetry to 'excite the collective imagination'. Once again, he is concerned about the dislocation of modern poetry from traditional culture. With good reason, he condemns the first literary modernists, Pound, Eliot, Joyce and Woolf for being élitist. 'Look for example, at a typical page of Ezra Pound's *Cantos* or the quotations at the front of *The Four Quartets* and you encounter an implicit disdain for the common reader'. Gone are the days when Tennyson was a best-seller. But Abbs' study of the poetry of Ted Hughes and R S Thomas, though highly critical, contains the hope that poetry may somehow flower again.

This is a remarkable collection of essays by a remarkable man. Abbs' passionate advocacy of cultural education springs from his own deprivation, and is all the more convincing because of its personal origins. Plato had his limitations as an educational authority; but at least the Greeks of the 5th century BC recognized that the arts were an essential part of education. A school education of the kind suffered by Abbs could not have occurred in ancient Greece. English society is still divided into two classes who scarcely communicate; those to whom the arts mean nothing, and those for whom the arts are so signally important that they cannot imagine life without them. Abbs has himself crossed this divide. I hope his book will persuade our rulers to ensure that more and more people are given the opportunity to do so by ensuring that the arts play their proper role in education.

Anthony Storr FRCP, FRCPsych., FRSL

SECTION ONE

Modernism and Post-Modernism

Contemporary culture is driven by the invisible engines of a market-economy and yet facing the deep questions of value and meaning the market-place is essentially blind. The arts in our century have also been hugely shaped by the powers of Modernism and Post-Modernism. At the moment Post-Modernism would appear to have triumphed, yet Post-Modernism often signifies little more than the triumph of simulacra over meaning, of surface over depth, of gloss over substance. Its work embodies the moral vacuum of the market economy. What is needed, then, is a critique of the unchecked market-economy and both the Modernist and the Post-Modernist movements. Perhaps the time has come to propose the primacy of the ethical and the aesthetic and to re-open the blocked channels between the arts and the primordial once again.

CHAPTER ONE

The Four Fallacies of Modernism

[handwritten annotations:] ideology — Historicism. prevailing zeitgeist
Social Protest (Scientism
Ethical Historicism — "clabism"

It is not easy to turn critically on Modernism for, in different ways, it has provided for many of us the very conditions of our perception and understanding. In its origins the Modernist movement seemed so liberating, so culturally and imaginatively demanding, that it is still difficult formally to recognize how in its later phases it became so sterile and imprisoning. This is because Modernism was never an object of our attention so much as the mode of our own sensibility. We saw through its eyes, spoke through its mouth, conceived through its mind. Just as one of Molière's characters suddenly realised that he had been speaking prose all his life, so we now realise that we *were* all Modernists, even without knowing it. But the realisation changes the phenomena, for it brings a critical distance and a new perspective. Once - it was only yesterday - it seemed that the artist was inevitably at the vanguard of civilisation, an innovator opening up the progressive forms of the future, an original and iconoclastic energy; once it seemed in the order of things that the arts in schools should deal with the contemporary, work only through 'process', remain 'relevant', be 'original' and wholly 'expressive'.

Today, we are less than sure. We turn on Modernism now and ask of it subversive questions. Why, for example, should the art-maker be conceived as always at the *vanguard of* civilisation? What is so valuable about endless experimentation? Why should innovation be valued almost as if it were a self-justifying aesthetic category? And, in the teaching of the arts, why should work be confined to 'process' or restricted to contemporary 'relevance'? In other words, we iconoclastically turn on the Modernist spirit. We ask subversive questions of the self-consciously subversive. We interrogate the dominant traditions of our century and find ourselves with a painful unease, on the outside, looking for better connections, concepts, possibilities; seeking not revolution but conservation, deep reclamation rather than innovation, continuities rather than disjunctions. *Bruckly!*

After a mere 80 years during which Art has hurtled through Expressionism, Fauvism, Dadaism, Cubism, Surrealism, Constructivism, Functionalism, Action Painting, Primitivism, Conceptualism, Minimalism, Kinetic Art, Op Art, Pop Art: where is there left to 'advance' to? After the '60s and '70s; after the electrocuting of fish in London galleries, after the covering of cliffs in polythene, after strutting for miles with a plank on your head, after filling the Tate Gallery with twigs and bricks and sand, after hanging up stained nappies and displaying Coca Cola bottles - what further possible innovation was left to the aspiring art-maker? Well, there *was* one gesture left, and there were artists and critics and gallery organizers ready to make and applaud it. Frank Kermode tells us in his essay 'Modernisms' that: 'Peter Selz, the Curator of Painting and Sculpture at the Museum of Modern Art was delighted with the famous *Homage,* which destroyed itself successfully, though not quite in the manner planned by the artist, before a distinguished audience'. But after that? What then? As the poet Leopardi said, *fashion is the mother of death* .

I believe Modernism had to end with its own destruction because it was informed by a number of false conceptions which have become more and more clear since its demise. I now want to explore the nature of those errors; I want to delineate what I conceive to be the four fallacies of Modernism. HISTORYCISM ⟩ p16 — ideologize

❂ The first fallacy relates to a concept of time, to a desire to escape the past and be of the moment. It is no accident that the word modernism derives from *modo,* meaning 'just now'. This desire for continuous modishness and 'advance' lay at the heart of Modernism and explains its current and inevitable exhaustion.

In 1965 the literary critic Leslie Fiedler wrote:

> Surely there has never been a moment in which the most naive as well as the most sophisticated have been so acutely aware of how the past threatens momentarily to disappear from the present, which itself seems to be disappearing into the future.

This expresses well the dizzy vortex created by the cumulative movements of Modernism, a sense of a pace which dissolved all that lay behind, in which there was no history, no continuity, no identity. The great black and white images of Kinetic Art, where all discrete parts flow into an endless motion *now,* symbolised perfectly this giddy

4

state of consciousness, of perpetual revolution, with no reference backwards, no cultural allusion, no hint of memory or of any historical past. How appropriate a symbol of Late Modernism the kinetic image is, creating an effect of endless movement based on the scientific principle of optics. Each period, it would seem, invents its own concept of historic time and literalises it, comes to read it in the succession of actual events, to experience it as an inexorable narrative dictating the forms of cultural life. Thus the Renaissance, envisaging itself as the rebirth of the Ancient World, erected the fiction of the 'Middle Ages'; the Enlightenment, considering itself the most illuminated period that had ever existed, reinvented those 'Middle Ages' as 'the Dark Ages'. Modernism has carried its own phantasy of time, its own story, in which the past is constantly and qualitatively superseded by the present moment. *Now,* according to this version of time, is always better than *then.* The ethical and aesthetic consequences of this concept have been, as we have slowly begun to realise, quite disastrous.

Ortega y Gasset unwittingly gave expression to this modernist concept of time as early as 1925 when he wrote:

> In art, as in morals, what ought to be done does not depend on our personal judgement; we have to accept the imperative imposed by the time.

In true modernist fashion Ortega continued:

> Obedience to the order of the day is the most hopeful choice open to the individual. Even so, he may achieve nothing; but he is more likely to fail if he insists on composing another Wagnerian opera, another naturalistic novel... In art, repetition is nothing.

In this configuration of assertions, we discern the heart of Modernist understanding. Fundamentally, it confers on what is conceived as inevitable historic progress the right to determine aesthetic practice and value. Such a view is seriously flawed for it assumes that History has a hidden teleology which can be discerned and which must determine aesthetic and ethical values. In each case we can turn on the interlocked assumptions and ask how History could possibly have such a teleological meaning and how, even if such an unwarranted assumption was held, one could be sure that one had grasped its meaning and finally, even if one granted the position, how it

5

but who sets the order of the day; whose imperative or the time bears?

could possibly dictate aesthetic and ethical criteria. One could, for example, paint convincingly *against* History and ethically act *against it* - as innumerable Jews must have felt they were doing in the 1930s against Hitler's version of historic destiny. In brief, History does not aesthetically justify Art.

Modernism was thus guilty of transferring the most dubious historic categories to realms where they did not belong. Its essential fallacy lay in a constant and insidious extrapolation of categories. *The modernity of art does not make it either aesthetically good or ethically valuable.* The value of art lies elsewhere; in its aesthetic power, in its vitality, in its relationship to the alert senses and the open imagination, deep in its own field of execution and reference. To say that something is contemporary is to tell us *nothing* of its *qualitative* value.

Yet such a simple fallacy had, like most fallacies, many destructive consequences. It led inevitably to the cult of constant change. In 1966 Morse Peckham wrote in *Man's Rage for Chaos* that:

> The conviction is almost universal that those who stick to obsolete beliefs and who refuse to change will go to the wall... that we must adapt or die.

So the cult of the new, in the post-war second phase of Modernism, led to movement after movement, fashion after fashion after fashion. In the 60s the practice of drawing from life, the practice of using paints and canvasses, the practice, even, of any kind of practice (for 'instant art' denied the need for any application) all but died. The cult of the contemporary made anything and everything possible.

The consequences of extreme Modernism become transparently clear in, for example, the following commentary by the art critic David Sylvester on the paintings of David Bomberg:

> Stylistically, Bomberg's later work was *backward looking,* added little or nothing to the language of art that had not been there 50 years before. If it is, as I believe, the finest English painting of its time, only its intrinsic qualities make it so: *in terms of the history of art it's a footnote.*

Note how the intrinsic painterly qualities are made unimportant. The history of art, according to this spurious and deadly logic, is that art must serve by constantly and quantitatively adding to its

6

technical repertoire. Here the central confusion of categories - the *imposition of the imagined historical on the actual aesthetic realm -* is unmistakably clear and its implications disturbingly visible. It is a good example of how art can disappear into the historic category and re-emerge as merely a footnote to an imagined social evolution.

Modernism, in brief, was guilty of what Karl Popper named 'historicism'. It saw itself as the inevitable outcome of the historic moment, the visible meaning of the assumed invisible imperative of history. Thus art has come to be seen and understood through an essentially alien category. It is more than likely when people now wander around modern galleries that they do not actually *see* the paintings but merely *conceive* them as 'contemporary art', as 'modern paintings', as 'the latest developments' in 'the history of art'. So people come to understand art discursively without ever aesthically responding to it! A curious state of affairs.

Many fallacies followed upon the historicist fallacy. I would like to enumerate three that have had profoundly destructive consequences on our understanding of art and of the teaching of the arts in our educational system. The first can be called *scientism.* As the Modernist movement developed, denying and destroying its own traditions, it became more and more prone, particularly in the visual arts, to adopt the language and assumptions of Science and Technology. After all, these intellectual disciplines seemed to be the true pace-setters, determining through another kind of relentless innovation, the forms of life to come. In Technology one could certainly talk, without ambiguity, of historical development and a kind of progress. Here the latest could claim, with some justification, to be, in fact, the best. Having denounced its past as obsolescent, many of the arts began to assimilate the language and the understanding of the theoretical and practical Sciences. Here lay a further alienation from the primary aesthetic experience. During the 60s and 70s some of the visual arts longed to join with the dominant technological force of their culture. This, too, must have seemed to many artists to be no more than a matter of historic necessity, of obeying the imperative of the prevailing *zeitgeist.*

Many of the manifestos of the 60s testify to the slip into the scientific and technological paradigm. Thus Frank Popper declared with philistine zest: 'Art will become an industrial product... . Art will become pure research like Science'. While the French artist

7

Vasarely claimed: 'From now on only teams, groups or whole disciplines can create: cooperation between scientists, engineers, technicians, architects and plasticians will be the *sine qua non* of the work of art'. It remains symptomatic that in many art colleges and in many school art courses today the work of the artist is labelled 'a mode of enquiry', a form of 'visual research', 'an assembling of data', a method of 'problem solving'. The language derives not from true art discourse, not from aesthetics, but from the illicit application of the methods and working assumptions of Science and Technology. Such language continues to mediate and perpetuate a form of aesthetic and cultural betrayal.

But scientism was not the only negative and distorting force in the theory of Modernism. There was also a related movement towards a *blank literalism*. Defending Robert Morris' *Slab* in the Tate Gallery, Michael Compton wrote in his introduction to the Arts Council brochure *Art as Thought Process:*

> At a certain level of consideration there is absolutely no ambiguity about such a sculpture as *SLAB* by Robert Morris. No matter how you look at it, it remains clear that it is just what was intended and at first glance just what you see.

A slab is a slab is a slab. Here lies the idea for another movement in art: SLABISM. But, of course, it is not necessary to invent. It came into existence under the name of Pop Art. As we know under this fashion, the objects of mass culture were simply reproduced and often endlessly repeated through photographic technique, as in Andy Warhol's *Marilyn Monroe* and *Coca Cola*.

One major tendency in Late Modernism has been to shift the contents of Woolworths or MacDonalds into the Guggenheim or the Tate and wholesale into Annual Exhibitions at the Hayward Gallery. In this 'tradition' the object of the art-maker was to reproduce the mass produced and insert it in a high-class institution. Without a real tradition, without prolonged apprenticeship, without the loving continuation and extension of traditional practices, such a dependence on the immediate commercial environment for symbolic material was, alas, all but inevitable.

The 'inspiration' of Pop Art was not exploratory or recreative. It was static and reproductive. The implication was: 'These things are real for contemporary society, therefore they should be the real objects

8

in art'. Invariably under such a rubric, art became a blind and bland extension of pop culture. It celebrated the same values: instant success, momentary fun, endless chop and change, brashness, casualness of style. Art became more ephemera, and mere ephemera, which was grotesquely fossilized when it was purchased and hung up in museums and galleries. The rapidity with which Lichenstein's 'blow-ups' came out of advertising and returned safely to it was amazing. Here was immediate relevance, an instant historic connection, a stunning contemporaneity: *GOT CHA! WHAM! WOW! BANG!*. Modernism, shunned and maligned in its early years, had under the influence of Pop Art become suddenly modish. Yet in Pop Art blankness merely reproduced itself, becoming, at best, social commentary of the most banal kind. The literal reproduction of things entails the imprisonment of the mind in those things and when they are spurious, then the mind is corrupted in the very process of faithfully reproducing them.

Pop Art, it was argued, was *a social protest.* And in this argument we perceive the third fallacy of late Modernism which is closely related to the historicist fallacy outlined earlier. It concerns *the overt and continuous politicization of the arts*. If art is secondary and History primary then art is most effectively judged through the historical and ideological dimension. This has happened in our own time on such a scale that we hardly notice its peculiarity. Ideological criticism forms the reigning orthodoxy. In the study of literature at University the dominant practice is to decode 'a text' in order to delineate its ideological content. Terry Eagleton would have all art measured against his own notion of 'real History', thus erecting a category of socio-political relevance as the final arbiter in literary judgement. John Berger, in a similar manner, brings overt political categories to bear directly on works of art. According to Peter Fuller:

> John Berger used to say that in front of pictures he always asked the question: 'How do these works help men and women to know, and to claim their social rights'.

How, one wonders, does such an ideological critic respond to Chagall's *Lovers in Lilac*, to Gwen John's sensitive cat paintings, to Henry Moore's archetypal *King and Queen*, to Cecil Collins's *The Sleeping Fool* or Keith Grant's *Sun Paintings?* What relevance do they have to the political class struggle? And, more fundamentally, why *should* they possess such political relevance? For art has its own deep transformative powers, its own interior meanings, its own aesthetic challenges.

The elevation of the historical category must lead not only to a radical misconception of the intrinsic purposes of art, but also to the triumph of an ideological criticism which seeks discursively to relate the manifestation of art to what is conceived as its primary historical meaning. Out of the cult of the historical emerges the omniscient critic whose function is to elaborate on what the art is *about,* relate it to its historic moment and provide its ideological interpretation. Thus, the intellectual eminence now given to the secular theologians of 'texts' and 'art objects'. The elevation of criticism brings about a further distancing from the aesthetic realm, for the question becomes not one of prolonged *aesthetic* engagement but one of *conceptual* meaning and the task, not one of creation or performance or appreciation, but simply of ideological judgement.

Underlying these various fallacies one senses the single fallacy of Historicism. For it is a belief in the historic 'now' which accounts for the shift into the scientific and technological, which explains the attraction of literally reproducing the dominant commercial world around us and which underlies the increasing and mediating power of ideological criticism. Having been so negative about late Modernism it is, perhaps, necessary that I briefly consider a way beyond the present state of exhaustion.

It is not possible to answer, quickly or easily, the question of what follows after Modernism. Perhaps such a question is in itself undesirably modernist in character. Here I can only hint at my complex feelings, realising that it is wrong-headed to dictate terms in advance of the necessary creative process. And one must realise, too, that art has many functions to serve. But I confess that over the next 50 years I would like to see artists having the audacity to go underground, to dig under the cement and tarmac of our modern cities, to bring up the buried images in order to reveal the deep abiding, contradictory, poetic forms of human life. I would like to see an archetypal art which greatly moved us, which shocked us, consoled us, affirmed us and which remained, at each turn and juxtaposition, faithful to the great tap-root of human existence. It would be strangely urgent and contemporary yet, also, hauntingly archaic. It would be committed to a further differentiation of the great images commensurate with

10

our own desolation. And if the vision was, in part, tragic it would yet confer depth and put an end to that great lie of the last 300 years, the lie of literal and inevitable progress. And, like all true art, it would take us beyond the unreal twilight of an exhausted materialism with its Scientisms, its Positivisms and its various Functionalisms. What I have in mind has been beautifully embodied in our century by a significant minority of art-makers; for example, in the art of Henry Moore, Cecil Collins (at his best as with his *Portrait of the Artist and his Wife, 1939*) and Frida Kahlo (at her most mythical) and in the musical work of Michael Tippett and John Taverner.

After Modernism there is nowhere to turn, but back and further back into our diverse historic cultures and down and further down into the depths of our existence, until the two tracks converge and become one. All this requires much greater elaboration. Here I would like to conclude with a reflection from the poet Oscar Milosz who claimed that few were daring enough 'to connect the time assigned to one human life with the time of all humanity', and who wanted symbols 'to penetrate to the very core of reality'. I would like to see an art grow up that was daring enough and comprehensive enough to create those deeply needed symbols.

(1987)

CHAPTER TWO

The Triumph and Failure of Post-Modernism

To understand the weaknesses of Post-Modernism (and its possible strengths) we must first understand Modernism. We must first put the fashionable movement into its broad historic context. As we saw in the last chapter, a clue to the understanding of Modernism is provided by the word itself. It derives from the Latin *modo* meaning literally *just now* and has obvious links with such related concepts as *modernity, modernisation, modish, a la mode.* The desire to be fully contemporary without reference to the cultural past and, particularly, the immediate past - the desire to be *just now* and fully of the moment - would seem to constitute the central commitment of most Modernists. By a curious paradox, deriving from a progressive view of historical development, the apparent brazen ahistoricity of much Modernism was based on a distinctive historical sense of its own need. Above all, most of the jostling and anxious avant-gardes often claimed to be serving 'the spirit of the time' (Hegel's term) as it moved into a necessary future.

In the middle of the 19th Century - in 1845 to be precise - the French critic Gabriel Desire Leverdent had written: 'Art, the expression of society, manifests, in its highest soaring, the most advanced social tendencies: it is the forerunner and the revealer. Therefore, to know whether art worthily fulfils its proper mission as initiator, whether the artist is truly of the avant-garde, one must know where Humanity is going, what the destiny of the human race is....' Without a doubt, the grand narrative here was shaped by an inexpugnable belief in an inevitable historical progress. Above all, what was involved was an open-eyed, intransient, forward orientation to future time. The guiding motto could have been lifted from Blake's *Proverbs of Hell* where it is written: 'Drive your cart and your plow over the bones of the dead'. We have to attempt to understand a vast international movement which was, at least in architecture and design, often devoted to the machine, to the idea and reality of mass-production and the

* French revolution, 'Salon', industrialization, Russia, Freud, Darwin, Dickens

notion of inevitable collective advance. Le Corbusier, for example, was to write in 1927 in *Towards a New Architecture:* 'Economic law inevitably governs our acts and our thoughts.... We must create the mass production of spirit'. There in one brief formulation we find both the notion of historic determinism (derived largely from Marx) and of the artist as functionary of the historic process, aiding and abetting it.

This insistence on a contemporaneity without reference to the past can be located in most of the manifestos and polemical declarations of the self-conscious Modernists. Marinetti directing the Futurists (a revealing title) wrote in 1909: 'but we will hear no more about the past we young strong Futurists'; Walter Gropius, founding father of the Bauhaus, that seminal centre of visual Modernism in design and mass-production, urged his students 'to start from zero'; while Mies Van der Rohe proclaimed a similar minimalist approach in his 'less is more'.

The insistence on iconoclastic originality, on continuous artistic experimentation, on the systematic disruption of the received codes created in the first flowering of Modernism an extraordinary vitality and arresting urgency. It gave birth to a series of memorable works: the dances of Isadora Duncan (between 1900-1920), Picasso's *Les Demoiselles d'Avignon* (1907), Matisses's *Dance* (1910), Stravinsky's *The Rite of Spring* (first performed in 1913, choreographed by Nijinsky and put on by Diaghilev's Russian Ballet Company), James Joyce's *Ulysses* (1922), T S Eliot's *The Waste Land* (also 1922), Kafka's *The Castle* (1926), then Virginia Woolf's *To the Lighthouse* (1927) and *The Waves* (1931). At the heart of much of this urgent and disturbing art was a crucial re-evaluation of the function of language in the arts, which was, in turn, a further extension of Romanticism. Artistic language was no longer seen as a received tool for a conventional and therefore confirming mimesis, but, rather, as a dynamic agent able through its own creative powers to explore and open up unconscious levels of reality and, therefore, human possibility, from nightmare unreality to visionary perception. The language aspires not to represent within fixed forms but to actively discover, to be prime agent of exploration.

Yet the imperative to 'keep it new' meant that one movement was destined to follow another, often with extraordinary rapidity. This was particularly true of the visual arts whose history provides us with the most unambiguous case of Modernism. Much of the restless

13

desire to experiment, to leap frenetically from one style to another, can be discerned in the prolific work of one great artist alone, namely, in the extraordinary *opus* of Picasso; but it can be detected, with little effort, across the span of the century in the sudden flowering and quick fading of a plethora of schools. In the early decades of this century it gave birth to Dadaism, Fauvism, Cubism, Futurism, Constructivism, Vorticism, to name only some of the more prominent movements.

As the century moved on, so the iconoclastic spirit became more frenetic and self-conscious. *The desire for revolution remained but artistically and culturally there was less and less to rebel against.* The last movement had done it all before. For the logic of perpetual revolution in the arts must lead, inexorably, to exhaustion. This was the story of Modernism. It depleted itself. Like a bad economy it systematically destroyed its resources and ended destitute. As time passed, it became not an authentic individual task but an international habit of mind, a kind of mind-set, a series of conventions against conventions, a tradition ironically against traditions. Certainly, by the 1960s, some of the more alert Modernists were aware of their own ironical position. The poet Octavio Paz, for example, declared that 'the avant-garde of 1967 repeats the deeds and gestures of those of 1917. We are experiencing the end of the idea of modern art'. If the systematic disruption of the received artistic codes engendered, in the first instance, remarkable acts of aesthetic exploration and vitality, it yet led, by a necessary self-depleting logic, to a state of anaesthetic exhaustion and bleak extremity almost entirely cut off from the community. It is also pertinent to notice that many of the great achievements of Modernism formed, as it were, symbolic *cul-de-sacs*, rather than bridges. No one was able to follow, with any success, the very peculiar achievement of T S Eliot's *The Waste Land,* Ezra Pound's *Cantos,* Joyce's *Finnegan's Wake,* not to mention the more iconoclastic examples of Duchamp's *Urinal* or John Cage's *4'33"* or whatever was the first example of Autodestruct 'art'. Their perverse extremity and wilful obscurity (the works show a relative contempt for any common audience and strike out against it) precluded any productive emulation. To a large extent they represent, in quite different ways, ends: dead-ends, culminations, denials, implosions. Modernism created the condition of its own impossibility until art became anti-art.

14

à l'art pour l'art ?

If this highly schematic and selective account of Modernism has any virtue it would suggest that it is necessary to differentiate between two stages of Modernism; its first highly creative substantive phase (from, say, 1900 to 1940) followed by its second decadent and rhetorical phase (from, say, 1940 to 1980). If the First World War marks the dramatic development of the first phase then the Second World War marks its demise and the emergence of the formulaic phase.

Doubtless, we are still too close to Modernism to define with justice its achievements and its failures or the reasons for its disintegration as *the* international 20th Century movement in the arts. *It is impossible for any account of such a labile, contradictory and multi-faced movement to be definitive.* Yet we need to ask, at least, two further questions. *Why did Modernism collapse around 1980? And what is the phenomenon of Post-Modernism which has claimed to take its place as the dominant cultural orientation of our own immediate time?*

As I have implied, I believe that international Modernism had to collapse because of its own tenets; the seeds of its own destruction lay within its own assumptions. This is not the place to locate all those assumptions; however as I argued in the last chapter the key fallacy, from which most of the others derive, is the fallacy of historicism and was defined by Karl Popper in *The Poverty of Historicism* (1957). What is meant by historicism in relationship to the Modernist movement in the arts? It entails an extrapolation of categories in which dubious historical terms are transferred into aesthetic terms and seen to justify various artistic movements and specific forms of art. The fallacy can be understood best by taking examples. Schaffer, a self-consciously Modernist painter, has claimed:

> Contemporary painting and sculpture don't interest me. Can you imagine anyone nowadays building a factory for the construction of horse-drawn carriages? Of course not! Well, it's the same with art: brushes were alright for painting and mallets for sculptures between the fourteenth and seventeenth centuries.

The argument depends upon a developmental view of history which is used to validate or invalidate and generally determine the form of artistic work. *That is precisely the fallacy of Historicism.* The supposed meaning of History (the march of historical events) is invoked to justify or disown values relating to the aesthetic and ethical domain.

15

Here is one further example taken from the columns of *The Independent*:

> In literature we have gone beyond Dickens and Tennyson, and in medicine and nursing beyond Joseph Lister and Florence Nightingale. Why should architecture alone among the arts and sciences turn its back upon innovation and change?
>
> (*William Rodgers, 7th September 1989*)

It is categorically and uncritically assumed that the artist has to be at the service of an inevitable historical development which both parallels and can be unambiguously measured by reference to stated technological advances. But it is fatuous to suggest that an author can go 'beyond Dickens' in the same way that medicine can be improved. Because it is modern, Centre Point is not aesthetically superior to the Parthenon. Often we have only to open our eyes to transcend the fallacies of historicism. Another aspect of historicism concerns the re-evaluation of art not aesthetically, but sociologically. If 'X' belongs to its time, then 'X' is valid. This critical approach, blind to the intrinsic artistic nature (or otherwise) of individual work, merely sees art as a *carrier of ideology*. Norman Rosenthal, for example, has recently described the function of the art-critic as follows: 'For as long as there are people around they will make those irrational things called art objects, and some of them will survive and become interesting *symptoms of our age*. My job is to try to recognize them.' (*The Independent*, 8th June 1991, my italics.) There, in all its naivety, lies the historical fallacy and with it the misreading of the nature of art: art as secondary symptom rather than as primary symbol.

Yet Modernism has relied heavily on this conception of historic advance. The very notion of the avant-garde, which as we have seen was one of the key terms in the lexicon of the international Modernist movement, entails the idea of being at the vanguard of the historical process and of serving 'the spirit of the age'. This preoccupation with progressive time is deep in Western culture but in the case of Modernism, it is derived largely from Hegel (1770-1831) and his subverting disciple Marx (1828-1883). The unclouded historic optimism of both Hegel and Marx fed the international Modernist movement with a sense of destiny - for who, in the age of dwindling religious faith, could possibly set themselves against the *meaning of history?* To be modern was to be on the crest of historic time; the task

16

was to be loyal to the moment, to the 'just now' of the imminent historic realization of 'the world spirit' (Hegel, in fact, thought history had ended in his own time, in 1806 to be precise) or the destined triumph of the proletariat and the subsequent withering away of the state.

The international disintegration of 'Communism' in the last few years must, surely, relate deeply to the final withering of the Modernist materialist ésprit? It is hard to understand how History could bear a pre-determined master narrative, and even if it did, how it would confer an absolute right to determine ethical or aesthetic principles. One can paint beautifully *against* 'the spirit of the age' - as some of our best British painters have done during the whole course of the Modernist Age. (Think of Paul Nash, John Piper, David Bomberg, Cecil Collins). With this realization, dramatically confirmed by the withering of Communism, we find ourselves now laying the spectre of Late Modernism and entering the emerging and uncertain ground of Post-Modernism; for Post-Modernism is a movement which consciously opens itself to the past, to the inexpugnable plurality of things and their expression as metaphor and ornament in our diverse human lives and plural cultures. It rejects any Utopian sense of the future and advocates a self-conscious reference to the past and the public memories and associations it carries. Post-Modernism negates Modernism by reversing that arrow of time. It is concerned to make playful ironic connections with the whole of the cultural continuum and has no faith in geometrical visions or singular necessities. It tends to be eclectic rather than uniform; ironic rather than revolutionary; conciliatory (even wanting to include its opponent through quotation) rather than iconoclastic. In his lucid monograph and manifesto *What is Post-Modernism?* Charles Jencks claims; 'I term Post-Modernism that paradoxical dualism, or double coding, which its typical hybrid name entails: the continuum of Modernism and its transcendence.' While Umberto Eco has written: 'The post-modern reply to the modern consists of recognizing that the past, since it cannot be fully destroyed, because its destruction leads to silence, must be revisited; but with irony, not innocently.' It is now time to look more closely at this fashionable cult of Post-Modernism.

Post-Modernism as a movement is, perhaps, only *dramatically* clear in the realm of architecture. There it is a spirited reaction against the international functionalism which through the various powerful

17

exponents of Modernism, from le Corbusier to Nikolaus Pevsner, had been widely hailed as the necessary architecture of all advancing industrial and technological societies. The Post-Modernist architects advocated against the monolithic style of rectangles and glass a self-conscious and ironic return to past traditions. As early as 1966 Robert Venturi - the architect of the fine Sainsbury's extension to the National Gallery - in *Complexity and Contradiction in Architecture* had urged a return to historical sources, proclaimed the values of elaboration, ambiguity and irony, and demanded an inclusive recognition of all previous cultural manifestations, both 'high' and demotic. This case was developed further by Charles Jencks in a stream of books, pamphlets and articles. According to Jencks, no 'present-tense architecture' was possible for there can be 'no escape from the historicity of language'. In essential agreement, J Mordaunt Crook wrote: 'the quest for objectivity in design has been very largely abandoned. We have had to re-learn what the nineteenth century painfully discovered: architecture begins where function ends'. And such architecture, given the heterogeneity of beliefs and communities, has for all Post-Modernists to be eclectic in character. From this perspective, Post-Modernism could be cogently represented as a kind of self-conscious cultural eclecticism.

Certainly, something of the Post-Modernist spirit, as manifested most visibly in contemporary architecture (in pitched roofs, in decorative motifs, in the use of local materials, in the affirmation of primary colours, in the eclectic use of the classical orders), is clearly at work in most other areas of our culture; in music, in the visual arts (particularly in the return to figurative and narrative art), in drama (where the place of the proscenium arch had been re-affirmed) and in much literature (where the practice of retelling and juxtaposing earlier narratives in the tradition has become almost the new literary orthodoxy). One thinks of writers such as Gabriel Garcia Marquez, Carlos Fuentes, Salman Rushdie and David Lodge - all of whom have been self-consciously preoccupied with notions of genre and ways of making problematic the nature of their subject matter. At the same time, in the teaching of the arts there is a growing recognition of the need to impart traditional expressive techniques and of the need to include more comprehensively the demanding artistic work from the cultural continuum. Such a commitment can be *loosely* associated with Post-Modernism as can the current nostalgia for

18

earlier periods, the development in our society of theme-parks and cultural heritage exhibitions and displays, together with the obvious popularity of faithful period reconstructions on film and television and, even, the widespread use of black and white images in television advertising. Looking back in anger has given way to looking back in nostalgia.

It is, also, clear that there are strong connections between Post-Modernism and Post-Structuralism as it has been developed in the work of the late Roland Barthes, Lacan, Derrida and Lyotard. All of these writers have expressed a strong opposition to the main categories of Western Philosophy from Plato to Marx. They have attacked what they see as the monolithic narrative of power which informs such notions as Progress, Truth, Beauty, Goodness and have stressed the polyphony of readings and symbolic possibilities that exist within the world of the sign. Jean Baudrillard, the much-vaunted champion and journalistic show-man of Post-Modernism, had taken the work of these thinkers to an extreme and declared: 'the simulacrum is true'. For Baudrillard (in as much as one can understand his abstract and *fuliginous writings) the signs we use no longer refer in the manner of the map or illuminate in the manner of the lamp, rather, under the power of the computer and the voracious mass media, they have become things in themselves, requiring (and possessing) no further justification. Baudrillard names the endless procession of simulacra without any referentiality 'the hyperreal'. Thus, in Post-Structuralism the accent falls on rhetoric (not truth) on appearance (not depth) and style (not content). The long search for truth in Western philosophy falls away as meaningless, the result of a naive misunderstanding of the nature of language which first began on a massive scale with Socrates and Plato. The affinity between these deconstructing philosophies and much of Post-Modernism is, as we shall see, astonishing for the artefacts of Post-Modernism would seem to say: there is only style, there is only internal reference within codes, the world is a quotation (within a quotation, within a quotation....). Nietzsche with his insistence that there could be no 'true world' only a play of 'perspectival appearances' was, without doubt, the fore-runner of the Post-Modernist creed.

It is at this point that some definitions and qualifications become necessary. In as much as Post-Modernism is used as a tag to denote the end of Modernism, to indicate a certain style in architecture and, more

* sooty,
dusky

broadly, to refer to a complex (often ironic) orientation to the past, it has a certain shorthand use. However, in as much as it defines a new movement in the arts *based on the spirit of the age,* it would seem to be often guilty of the same fallacy as Modernism, namely a kind of Historicism. *And what must come after Modernism in the arts?* This is a question predicated on the historicist fallacy. And it is a false question. For no more than Modernism can the term Post-Modernism confer aesthetic worth or ethical value. At best, it can define a set of practices and conventions which can be used well or badly.

Charles Jencks has written that 'the characteristic fact of life in an age of information processing is a reworking of previous traditions'. The Post-Modern age, he claims, depends on the advent of organised knowledge, world communication and cybernetics. Because our age is plural 'no orthodoxy can be adopted without self-consciousness and irony'. As we listen to the phrases and demands we begin to hear the drum-beat of the characteristic Modernist manifesto committed, once again, to the spirit of the age. We encounter a theory linked to a historic unfolding which is seen to determine the nature and the mood of art-making. Post-Modernism, ironically enters as the imperious avant-garde after Modernism. It, too, is seen as part of the zeitgeist. It becomes the next fashionable movement after it had been said there could be no more 'nexts'. A continuation of Modernism by other means!

The informing historicism comes out clearly in the following quotations from Charles Jencks' *What is Post-Modernism?* Jencks claims that it is an 'information age' which creates the necessary aesthetics of post-modernity:

> The Post-Modern Age is a time of incessant choosing. It's an era when no orthodoxy can be adopted without self-consciousness and irony because all traditions seem to have some validity. This is partly a consequence of what is called the information explosion, the advent of organized knowledge, world communication and cybernetics.

The information revolution is seen as engendering and justifying the eclectic and inclusive aesthetic with its ironic, cosmopolitan, self-conscious disposition. 'Once a world communication system and form of cybernetic production have emerged they create their own necessities', writes Jencks; and continues 'they are, barring a nuclear war, irreversible'. But in tone this sounds remarkably like the earlier

& 'anything goes'.

Le Corbusier in 1927, except that the new imperative is not 'the mass production spirit' but an ironic pluralism.

Is it possible that, in its turn, Post-Modernism is creating not an exacting living culture, but a hall of reflecting mirrors, another wasteland decorated with plaster-cast motifs and plastic gods; a culture confined to bright surfaces and facile allusions? Certainly, like billboard advertising, many of its expressions seem less than a millimetre thick; and there is nothing behind the surface for Post-Modernism (like Post-Structuralism) eschews metaphysical and grounded meaning. And while it glances back to historic cultures, it does so with a superior smile - for *irony* is always superior to whatever it puts itself into relationship with. In *Back to the Future* Philip Cooke talks about Post-Modernist architecture as being an art which 'entertains as it parodies *the pretensions of the past*' (my italics). The description is deeply revealing. In its cultivated *superiority to the past* it strongly echoes the Modernism it claims to challenge. The past is not so much read, as raided; it is seen as a book of motifs, not as a living source. Thus, while International Modernism constructed a world of monolithic monotony, its reactive offspring is building a rainbow-like palace, with gothic arches mounting supermarket counters and temple pillars masking mundane offices. The symbolism adapts to the market place and, in a bright explosion, perishes there.

It is true that Post-Modernism is delightfully free of the heavy spirit of literalism and functionalism. It is the very antithesis of conceptualism; the exuberant opposite of minimalism. It *does* engage with memory; it *does* invite imaginative play; it *recognizes* community and relishes the aesthetic wealth of material (both natural and artificial, both local and international). All of these elements are of value, yet so often looking at its works one is often left with a sense of the facile, a symbolic show, a display of references, where all values hang in quotation marks and where nothing is spiritually earned. A very clever game is being played, but there is an absence of interiority and profundity.

'We now have the luxury of inheriting successive worlds as we tire of each one's qualities', proclaims Jencks. But it is precisely here that we encounter the problem. While the Post-Modernist may emulate all, he believes in none. He is the symbolic opportunist of all time; the Don Giovanni of every possible 'taste culture', sampling each but committed to none. What does this ultimately represent but a form of international aestheticism (the very word 'luxury' is indicative) which conceals its own inner bankruptcy through a dazzling display of borrowed signs and quotations? Perhaps the irony, which is insisted on as the distinctive characteristic, is already an expression of exhaustion and an unconscious defence against it? What happens when the cultural globe-trotter grows weary? At that point does he return to confront the spectre of nihilism which Nietzsche saw as a sign of our own century? And what then?

In coming to terms with Post-Modernism we need to consider the limitations of irony. Can a cultural renaissance, such as Jencks calls for, be based on irony? Is it sufficient? Irony is an excellent corrosive agent; it empties out; it distances; it makes duplex and frees the mind from the literal and the factual. It allows for an aerial play of mind, an intelligent levity of spirit. But of itself, has it the power to create compelling artistic work or provide the fundaments of civilization? If 'only the simulacrum is true', then only simulation is left. And if we are to judge this simulacrum by the painters espoused by Charles Jenks in his monograph *What is Post-Modernism* - the painters of ultimate pastiche and futile replication, Carlo Maria Mariani, Robert Longo, David Salle and Stone Roberts - we must regard the achievement as negligible, lacking in all painterly quality and devoid of imagination. Simulation is, simply, not good enough.

For all its much hyped innovation and its vaunted audacity the Post-Modernist style is, ultimately, that of the ornamental ironic or of the ironic Baroque. Post-Modernism tethers the power of passion and makes neutral all values, casting all creation into the single mould of irony and cleverness. The angels it favours are angels of pantomime, light, smiling, ornamental, plastic; they are not the compelling angels of Giotto, Rilke or Cecil Collins; they do not begin to possess their transcendent gravity or their promise of ineffable possibility. Free from moral and metaphysical commitment, wedded only to parodic imagination, Post-Modernism hovers like a transient rainbow over the abyss. And like a rainbow it cannot last.

As a philosophy for the arts, Post-Modernism must be stringently queried. It is for individual artists, in relationship to their gifts and their own particular visions of the world, to create significant art, *for or against or beyond the spirit of the age*. It is for the critic and for the audience to evaluate it. What we need is not a fashionable theory based on a questionable reading of history, and merely fitting the present consumer society, but a better recognition of the primacy of the aesthetic and ethical. We need to recognize the profound freedom of the artist to embody his or her apprehensions of meaning and value. Once again, the artistically liberating position outlined by Hart Crane in 1930, that the artist exists to articulate through the power of metaphor the nature of human consciousness *sub specie aeternitatis,* needs urgent attention.

(1993)

CHAPTER THREE

Post-Modernity and the Teaching of the Arts

Culturally we are now living in a Post-Modernist, Post-Marxist, Post-Progressive age. For many arts teachers, who for the best part of the century have worked in a cultural matrix determined by these three vast and interacting ideologies, this may seem a negative and deeply depressing state of affairs. There is a sense of quiet - or not so quiet - outrage among many arts teachers. This outrage (some of it, politically highly justified) needs now to become not reactive but profoundly and productively reflective. Could it be that the virtual demise of the three ideologies offers space for a necessary rethinking and practical re-orientating of aesthetic practice - a rethinking of the place of art and arts teaching, not only in terms of the national curriculum but in terms of the next century? Quite simply the intellectual vacuum around us calls for a deep revisioning of the arts. It is a mistake to clutch on to notions which cluster around such verbal tags as 'bourgeois art', 'elitist culture', 'self-expression', 'multi-cultural education', 'relevant', 'child-centred', 'topics', 'themes', 'process learning', 'problem solving' and, of course, all the unspeakable jargon of 'managerial-speak', manufactured and delivered by a government which has lost the capacity to think *educationally* about education or *culturally* about culture and that without any sense of shame can link the arts to tourism, pleasure, leisure and the corrupt symbolism of the admass machine.

What is so disorientating is that even in the teaching of the arts we have often failed to develop a resonant language based on *aesthetics,* on a long historic culture and on the primacy of the imagination. In particular, we have not valued the place of the cultural continuum sufficiently nor the place of European culture in whose symbolically depleted habitat we now struggle to breathe. This has been true of *nearly all the arts in education* during the whole course of the 20th Century. Here, for example, is Malcolm Ross in 1989 describing his own work: "We were not after all advocating education in the arts - still less an apprenticeship for school children in the high Western artistic tradition. Real art and real artists were all but incidental to the thesis of human expressivity that the project was advancing." Human expressivity is here placed almost *against* the intelligence of art and the intelligence of the cultural continuum. That has been the dominant tune of decades of arts teachers and arts educators. But is it good enough? It is deep enough? Is it coherent enough?

The black American writer Toni Morrison talking about her novel *Jazz* said recently: "People think the past is something you can romanticise and which threatens you. I think of it as something which walks along with you. I know I can't change the future but I can change the past. Insight and knowledge change the past. It is the past, not the future, which is infinite. Our past was appropriated. I am one of the people who has to re-appropriate it." This creative relationship with a living and constantly changing past and its implications for arts teaching is my theme and one essential aspect is the notion of a *democratic and radical re-appropriation of it.*

Western civilization does not belong, by some divinely inspired *fiat,* to any one group or class in society. It belongs to all those who consciously and unconsciously grapple with its immense preoccupations, its cultural achievements, its moral failures, its contradictions, its neuroses, its dynamic potentialities, and its long and ennobling concern with freedom, with justice, with equality and with the desire for existential meaning, from Socrates to Sakharov from Sappho to Sylvia Plath. Western civilization *is* our complex cultural home. Any aesthetic developed outside that home is bound to be muddily provincial, merely contemporary, spuriously international or thinly and patronisingly multi-cultural.

As Toni Morrison indicates, a romantic and nostalgic view is as unproductive as a paranoid and defensive view. What *is* required is a tough and discriminating view, one that looks for lines of continuity (as much as discontinuity) for analogues and parallels (as much as differences); one searching out and repossessing artistic forms, techniques, narratives, grammars which, in a contemporary context, can become the means for further imaginative transformation and renewal. Bertolt Brecht once wrote in good Marxist fashion: "... the conduct of those before us is alienated from us by an incessant evolution". Now *that* expresses an alienation from the cultural continuum which defines the challenge for the next century.

The truth is that most of the great cultural movements of the past have gone back to step forward. The Renaissance discovered the Greeks; the Romantics returned to the Gothic; Jung's analytical psychology excavated alchemy. History is not an arrow and there is no predetermined target. The poetics we need are relational and ecological, not linear and progressive; pespectival and not singular. We need now to reconnect, in complex and demanding ways, with the whole of the cultural continuum. Ironically, Modernism is now *one* tradition (much of it in its later phases spiritually trite).

Toni Morrison suggests a radical reappropriation of our past. I would link that to a certain kind of artistic Post-Modernity which reclaims the past and *puts it to contemporary use*. I am thinking of the subversive art of retelling: Abraham's readiness to burn his son but told from Isaac's point of view; Miranda without a Prospero; Robinson Crusoe but re-defined by the 'savage' Man Friday. Such retellings do not have to be ironic; they can be moral, passionate and compelling. What is required, though, is a knowledge of metaphors, parables, grand narratives and the power to artistically and philosophically refract, subvert and, even, invert them. But there is another relationship to the past which I think must co-exist (with great tension and a certain discomfort) with this and is the necessary condition for its existence.

The position I am referring to has been put forward most eloquently by the philosopher Michael Oakeshott. In a paper entitled *Learning and Teaching* he wrote:

> To initiate a pupil into the world of human achievement is to make available to him much that does not lie upon the surface of his present world. The business of the teacher (indeed, this may be said to be his peculiar quality as an agent of civilization) is to release his pupils from servitude to the current dominant feelings, emotions, images, ideas, beliefs, and even skills, not by inventing alternatives to them which seem to him more desirable, but by making available to him something which approximates more closely to the whole of his inheritance.

The present, in this way of looking, is what is alienated (think, for one moment, of the torrent of increasing triviality which thunders down on our heads, day after day, and you may feel inclined to concede the point) *and the past potentially liberating*. In this reading of time and culture, Homer, Shakespeare, Rembrandt, Mozart *read us* and

26

we find ourselves and our daily ephemeral assumptions thereby challenged by the power of their individual and collective voices. Through engaging with their narratives and images we can gain a critical perspective on our own age which is liberating. We can become through a conversation across the generations agents of a long reflexive civilization, and in this way free ourselves from the tyranny of quick ideologies and consumer fads. This means that in the teaching of the arts we need touchstones more than themes, exemplars rather than topics. The aim is the creative initiation of the child into the best of the received culture.

reflexive civilization

anchors role models

There are two dynamic views of cultural time here and they are somewhat oppositional - but I think we need both and, that the dialectical current of Western Culture is made up of both: *a kind of piety to ancestors and also a turbulent iconoclastic spirit, infinitely restless, infinitely searching, infinitely dissatisfied.* The Classical and Romantic; the Apollonian and the Dionysian. We need to be able to submit ourselves to the intrinsic qualities of great works of art across time; but we need to preserve, simultaneously, the freedom to change, to subvert, to tell again with a different outcome. In re-appropriating a culture we discover, with elation, those metaphors which illuminate and extend, but we also, inevitably, encounter metaphors which restrict, which cage, which damage; and these need to be cast again in the human imagination according to our own sense of the truth, however precarious. It is these new narratives, resonant with the past but oppositional in meaning, which can forge the keys to unlock the cage and release the entrapped and unhappy personages. Exit Rapunzel from her tower. Exit Isaac as the silent victim of the father. Exit the wife Xanthippe from the logical conundrums of Socrates.

Pinkola – Estès Pandora

Here, then, are two views of historic culture, the conservative and the subversive. In the first view, the cultural continuum offers us work which challenges us, educates us, expands us. It is our fine inheritance. In the second it offers us material to be endlessly refashioned, raided, rectified, reformulated. It is our eclectic workshop. As arts educators we should struggle to include both views - so that we cultivate in our pupils an imagination which attends to the intrinsic nature of works of art and which yet feels free to recast their forms, their narratives and their moral outcomes. As arts teachers it is our task to create both *careful readers and piratical raiders*.

How does such an approach relate to the National Curriculum?

While the structures which have been wilfully imposed on the arts are not just (the exclusion of drama as an arts discipline and the fusion of dance with PE remain scandalous) and their conceptions of learning not sufficiently dynamic, they *do* have the merit of generally relating to historic culture. *The Order for Music in the National Curriculum* urges, for example, that pupils recognise the traditions of Indian raga and Indonesian gamelan and respond to composers from Tallis to Tippett. While *The Order for Art* suggests, for example, that the teacher takes the archetypal theme of 'Mother and Child' across different kinds of art such as 'icons, sculptures of Henry Moore, the paintings of Leonardo da Vinci and Mary Cassatt and African tribal art'. Engagement with the whole cultural field is insisted upon. As far as it goes, that is good.

What is essential, though, is that arts teachers refuse any temptation to teach the tradition *mechanically* (that would throw us back a hundred years); what is needed is for teachers to release the energies inherent in good art into the creative imagination where it can be contemplated and loved or turned again into new narratives and new challenges or, as I have implied earlier, both of these in due order. As teachers of the arts we need also to keep together the act of appreciation and the act of creation. And it is here in this reciprocal movement between the two activities that we need access to both the seemingly oppositional views of cultural time: to both piety before ancestors (so that we are ready to learn from them) and that subverting spirit which seeks to challenge, to retell, to ask again. For it is in this endless dialectic that education, both aesthetic and critical, takes place; and it is our task as teachers to keep it alive.

(1993)

The Nature of Aesthetic Education

In our society we have failed to develop any adequate public conception of the true significance of the arts. They exist not necessarily on the margins but always in an indeterminate state, constantly distorted by extraneous demands, curious expectations and fundamental misunderstandings. Under the controlling forces of a market economy the arts are invariably placed under the banner of leisure and consumption; they become commodities, competing with other commodities in the hustle and bustle of the market place. In education, similarly, they are misplaced and misunderstood, not generally envisaged as possessing the same value as the Humanities and Sciences. The essays gathered in this section define an alternative conception of the arts as indispensable vehicles for the development of consciousness without which any concept of the good society would be impossible.

CHAPTER FOUR

On the Value and Neglect of
the Arts in Education

Nietzsche claimed that in life 'we must enlist rather than resist those magnificent monsters, the passions'. I believe that our schools for the most part resist the passionate energies and engage, at best, only certain parts of the human psyche, the passive intellect and the recording memory. Our schools are still based on an inert and outmoded concept of knowledge as facts 'out there' unsullied by human consciousness. Thus education is still largely conceived as transmission of information from the teacher (as neutral medium) to the pupils, information which then has to be dutifully recorded by the learners and, through either writing or verbal parroting, returned to the teacher. An 'objective' process.

I want to address the following question. Why have we developed a notion of knowledge, and therefore of education, which excludes passion, fantasy, intuition, feeling, hunch, apprehension, doubt, belief, impression, dream, vision and the symbolic forms through which these powers or states of being can be explored and elaborated, given form, structure and living coherence? To put the question another way, why have we evolved a notion of knowledge which takes no account of the knowledge of the poet, the artist, the composer, the dancer, for surely their symbolic forms are there for common inspection and represent ways of knowing and being-in-the world? A brief historical answer to this question must be attempted. After that, I will return to the positive assumption in the last questions - namely, to consider why the arts are so important, and how an initiation into their various languages could enhance human life and suggest a way forward.

In the West since the disintegration of the Medieval world-picture there have developed two powerfully dominant schools of philosophy, Continental Rationalism and Anglo-Saxon Empiricism. Both, because of their informing assumptions, could find no place for the various expressive cultural forms. Both schools developed a concept of knowledge in harmony with scientific exploration, and the innumerable discoveries and inventions of science seemed further to confirm the truth of the philosophical concepts. With the Industrial Revolution, which was, from this perspective, the social incarnation of these theories, the informed conceptions of the few slowly became the commonplaces of the many, so that today there is a widespread assumption that scientists and experts *know*, and that if problems are a matter of feelings they are 'merely subjective', and that in life we should always look for 'hard facts' and be 'objective'. (We do not talk about 'hard' or 'solid' feelings, nor do we talk about 'mere' objectivity.)

) Let us turn, first, to the Rationalist tradition. It was Kepler who lucidly gave expression to their faith in quantities and numbers. 'The mind', Kepler declared, 'has been formed to understand not all sorts of things, but quantities, the further a thing recedes from quantities the more darkness and error inheres in it'. Spinoza sought to understand man by reference to 'lines, planes and bodies'. Descartes, in his *A Discourse on Method,* tells us that 'I reckoned as well nigh false all that was only probable'. Behind this almost fanatical quest for absolute certainty was a mathematical concept of knowledge. Descartes writes:

> The long chains of simple and easy reasonings by means of which geometers are accustomed to reach the conclusions of their most difficult demonstrations had led me to imagine that all things, to the knowledge of which man is competent, are mutually connected in the same way.

Descartes did not question the mathematical model. He assumed that what was logically necessary was also true in the sense that it also must refer to truths about life. But the crucial point is that, given such an informing conception of knowledge - that truths can only be established through long chains of simple reasoning - then nearly all the main expressive forms developed to find meaning and orientation in the world are relegated to a shadowy region. There is no aesthetics in Descartes' work, no philosophy of culture, nor could there be. In the opening autobiographical chapter of *A Discourse of Method* Descartes, examining his own education, maintains that history can never 'represent the truth', must always contain some fictions and exaggerations, and that poetry - in order, presumably, to make up for its lack of logical order - 'has its ravishing graces and delights'. Poetry, Descartes indicates, is concerned with 'the most agreeable fancies', and, having said so much, he quickly turns to mathematics, praising 'the evidence and certitude of their reasonings'. If, as the philosopher held, we can only arrive at the most important truths through the reasoned building up of clear ideas, then history, the study of past cultures, can have little value and *the arts no central place in the task of understanding, in the curriculum of the mind.* And yet Descartes did not stop to consider that the very clear thoughts he expounded might depend upon the language he used, that such thoughts as 'cogito ergo sum' might be impossible in many languages, and that if such 'universal truths' could only be mediated through certain languages there might be a problem about their universality. His thinking was ahistorical, acultural, and constituted a flight from the human world. Inevitably, it has had disastrous consequences for the human world and, particularly, for the arts.

Descartes' definition of the self makes, by all that it excludes, the general dilemma clear:

> I thence concluded that I was a substance whose whole essence or nature consists only in thinking and which, that it may exist, had need of no place, nor is dependent on any material thing; so that *I,* that is to say, *the mind by which I am what I am*, is wholly distinct from the body, and is even more easily known than the latter.

Given such an ontology, a concept of the self as pure mind, then there can be no place for the culture of the feelings or the culture of the senses, and, least of all, a place for the concept of wholeness, of heart and mind running harmoniously together.

The passage also reveals the rift which Descartes established in his philosophy between mind and matter: the mind as self stood on one side; on the other, the physical universe, including the body of man. On the physical side everything could be explained in terms of *matter* and *motion.* As with the wax he scrutinises in *Meditations on the First Philosophy,* so with the world, all that 'out there' is 'nothing, except something extended, flexible, and moveable', a world devoid of colour, taste, smell, texture and, at a different level, informing purpose. The primary qualities of the material universe are mechanical and mathematical. It was under this conception of nature that science made so many of its discoveries. The fact that the theory was practically productive made it seem infallible. The philosophy of mechanism prevailed, and tended to forget the problem of the cogito, the self locked in the machine.

In Descartes, in Galileo, Kepler and the great Renaissance scientists and philosophers began that scientific revolution which cast into the darkest shadow the full symbolic energies of man. The traditional symbolism in which man and universe corresponded, in which the human form was also the form of nature (microcosm-macrocosm), in which life was regulated by the fixed stars and the fixed stars regulated by life, was slowly eroded. The traditional double vision turned into the modern single vision. Before the Renaissance many symbols had a double reference, scientific and spiritual, intellectual and emotional. What happened under the mechanistic theories of Descartes and Galileo was that much of the symbolism was taken over and the subjective element progressively eliminated. The symbols were reduced to signs possessing single unambiguous meanings which could be systematically used to chart the nature of the external world. There can be little doubt that under this revolution a truer picture of the universe developed. At the same time this great advance in understanding of the outer tended to eclipse the inward world of consciousness. As a result, the inner came either to be understood in terms of the outer or even denied. This tendency reached its peak, perhaps, in nineteenth-century materialism. Taine, for example, under the power of the scientific vision, could write 'vice and virtue are products just as sulphuric acid and sugar are' and 'today, history, like zoology, has found its science of anatomy'. Many of the humanities still yearn for the order of the natural sciences, an order which would seem quite out of keeping with the content of their disciplines.

The gradual effacing of all the symbolic images which man had thrown over the cosmos, giving it human order, drama and meaning, created in the most sensitive individuals an immediate sense of anguish, a feeling of deep loss. Pascal, a contemporary of Descartes, himself an important scientist, inventor, and mathematician, recorded this experience of cosmic loneliness again and again:

Everywhere I see only infinities, which enclose me like an atom, like a shadow which lasts only an unreturning instant.
When I consider the short span of my life, absorbed in the eternity

34

preceding, the eternity following, the little space I fill, and even that space I see swallowed up in the infinite immensity, of spaces I know not, which know not me, I am astonished and terrified to see myself here rather than there, for there is no reason why it should be here rather than there, why now rather than then.

The new space opened up by science left the individual surrounded by a nature which had become morally indifferent to his fate and which was symbolically empty. Marjorie Grene, considering Galileo's conception of the universe (a conception very close to that of Descartes) wrote:

It is not only poetry in the narrow sense, the craft of making verses, that is here exiled from reality, but the whole work of imagination: myth and metaphor, dream and prophecy. In the bare mathematical bones of nature there is truth, all else is illusion. Yet that 'all else' includes the very roots of our being, and we forget them at our peril.

The passage can stand as our conclusion to this brief study of Rationalism, for it is myth, metaphor, dream and prophecy *and the state of mind which underlies them* that we would wish to restore to our impoverished state-school curriculum. If we are to do this we need a much broader framework than the Rationalist tradition can provide. Yet the narrowness of our curriculum is, I believe, in part, an expression of the Empiricist tradition which we must now glance at.

2) The Empiricist tradition, while believing more in the inductive method and in the construction of our conception of the world through sense perception, was likewise committed to the remarkable advances of science. John Locke wrote in his influential *An Essay Concerning Human Understanding*:

The commonwealth of learning is not at this time without master-builders, whose mighty designs, in advancing the sciences, will leave lasting monuments to the admiration of posterity: but every one must not hope to be a Boyle or a Sydenham; and in an age that produces such masters as the great Huygenius and the incomparable Mr Newton, with some others of that strain, it is ambition enough to be employed as an under-labourer in clearing the ground a little, and removing some of the rubbish that lies in the way to knowledge.

The modest, meek and deferential tone towards science charact-erised the tradition of Empiricism, and is a measure of its philosophical position. The contemporary philosopher Quine, faithfully echoing this whole school of thought, recently announced, that as far as he was concerned, philosophy and the philosophy of science were one and the same thing. It is easy and dangerous to over-simplify - but it would not seem a gross distortion to say that the Empiricist tradition culminated in a very simple distinction which was applied with inexorable logic to every facet of life. The distinction was between a verifiable and an unverifiable utterance. If an utterance was verifiable, then it could be established by public and empirical procedure as being true or false. If it was unverifiable, it meant that there was no clear way of establishing and testing the evidence, and that it was either logically confused or emotive, a private judgement which one either liked or disliked. Aesthetic and cultural evaluations were seen to belong to the unverifiable category, and nothing meaningful could be said about them. The role of philosophy thus came to be that of analysis, of classifying and clarifying *and* cleansing. The philosopher became a language-technician, 'an under-labourer in clearing the ground a little and removing some of the rubbish that lies in the way to knowledge'.

With the Empirical tradition we find, again, a closed circle in which the language and experience of the arts can find no entry. If aesthetics is a matter of private whim and fancy, and not also a way of knowing, relating and existing, then the arts are impoverished and reduced to the level of wine-tasting, or, as Bentham actually implied, push-pin. And, as with the Rationalist tradition, we also notice a philosophy which excludes not only feeling but also the whole confused mass of hunches, interpretations, intuitions, doubts, beliefs, fantasies which constitute our actual experience. The tradition of Empiricism slices off nearly all the contents of consciousness and casts them into oblivion, leaving only a tiny segment which can be meaningfully analysed. It was inevitable, then, that this tradition would devalue the arts just as much as the Rationalist tradition.

Some pertinent criticism of Empiricism came from within itself (although it went largely unheeded) in John Stuart Mill's *Autobiography* and in his brilliant essay on Coleridge and Bentham. In the latter essay his description of Bentham can be seen not only to focus on the limitations of the man but also of the philosophy be held:

36

He had never been made alive to the unseen influences which were acting on himself, so consequently on his fellow creatures. Other ages and nations were a blank to him for purposes of instruction. He measured them by but one standard; their knowledge of facts, and their capability to take correct views of utility, and merge all other objects in it. He saw accordingly in man little but what the vulgarest eye can see; recognised no diversities of character but such as he who runs may read. Knowing so little of human feelings he knew still less of the influences by which those feelings are formed: all the more subtle workings both of the mind upon itself, and of external things upon the mind, escaped him; and no-one probably, who, in a highly instructed age, ever attempted to give a rule to all human conduct, set out with a more limited conception either of the agencies by which human conduct *is*, or of those by which it *ought* to be influenced.

Mill's autobiography marks a more personal attempt to transcend the limitations of Bentham's philosophy as understood and imposed on him by his father, James Mill. In the one remarkable chapter of an otherwise dry and fact-obsessed autobiography, Mill describes his attempt to transcend his own lopsided cognitive development. In that chapter he dramatically defends the importance of the until then suppressed power of feeling:

The maintenance of a due balance among the faculties now seemed to me of primary importance. The cultivation of the feelings became one of the cardinal points in my ethical and philosophical creed. And my thoughts and inclinations turned in an increasing degree towards whatever seemed capable of being instrumental to that object.

In Wordsworth's poems Mill found the integration of thought and feeling which he was in search of. But the meaning of this integration was never worked out in philosophical terms. Indeed, as Mill's own autobiography would seem to testify, the philosopher never achieved this integration himself, and so the English tradition of philosophy moved forwards unaltered by Mill's critical break-down, and all that it so obviously symbolised about the disassociation of thought and feeling. Whether philosophy was conceived as the accumulation of well-tested and verified facts *or* as the application of mathematical logic in order to clarify the workings of the world, in both cases the arts were accorded no value, and all the elusive qualities which make up our daily experience of life denied or undermined. The success of these schools of philosophy has, I believe, helped to secure an educational system which invariably places fact over feeling, object over subject, reason over imagination and seems incapable of labouring for their proper integration. In the following passage from the philosopher David Hume the two schools can be seen coming lethally together, and all that does not meet their strict and simple criteria is thrown like so much offensive rubbish to the flames:

> When we run over libraries by these principles what havoc must we make? If we take in our hand any volume, or divinity or school metaphysics, for instance, let us ask, *does it contain any abstract reasoning concerning quantity or number?* No. *Does it contain any experimental reasoning concerning matter of fact and existence.* No. Commit it then to the flames for it can contain nothing but sophistry and illusion. (my italics)

We can find both the sources and the counterparts of Rationalism and Empiricism in Greek philosophy. Plato believed in the powers of mathematical reason. His ideal forms, existing outside nature, imperishable and perfect, possess the enduring immobility of geometrical constructions. Aristotle, breaking away from Plato and establishing his own methods, laid the foundations of empirical science, continually insisting that every hypothesis be tested by all the available evidence and recognising the need for constant collection and systematic classification. Yet, at the same time, both philosophers *were* concerned with the nature of the arts and the influence they exerted on human life. Neither of them doubted the attractive and dramatic energies of music, myth, drama, art or denied their power to order, change, enhance or degrade life. Both men were convinced that the arts could exert a formative influence on behaviour. In *The Laws* Plato even concerns himself with the particular rhythm with which the mother should rock the child - for good rhythm is harmony, and harmony (for Plato) is akin to moral goodness. Aristotle, for similar reasons, urges that music should be a vital part of the curriculum because 'music has a power of forming the character and should therefore be introduced into the education of the young'.

The most positive development of this theme is found in Book III of Plato's *Republic*. According to Herbert Read, author of the influential *Education Through Art,* some of the passages contain all the crucial points in his own plea for an aesthetic approach to the curriculum. The following excerpt takes us to the heart of Plato's argument:

Socrates
'Then beauty of style and harmony and grace and good rhythm depend on simplicity, - I mean the true simplicity of a rightly and nobly ordered mind and character, not that other simplicity which is only an euphemism for folly?'
'Very true', he replied.
'And if our youth are to do their work in life, must they not make these graces and harmonies their perpetual aim?'
'They must.'
'And surely the art of the painter and every other creative and constructive art are full of them - weaving, embroidery, architecture, and every kind of manufacture; also nature, animal and vegetable - in all of them there is grace or the absence of grace. And ugliness and discord and inharmonious motion are nearly allied to ill words and ill nature, as grace and harmony are the twin sisters of goodness and virtue, and bear their likeness.'

Plato is here asserting that if we make the rhythmic arts the basis of education, then we develop in the young a sense of form and style, a grace in being, which is also the mark of moral goodness. In the subsequent elaboration of this key idea, Plato contends that such an education, such an active intuition into the forms of beauty, would also draw, imperceptibly, the young towards 'the beauty of reason'. Aesthetic education is the preparation for a wider education, leading out into rational understanding and moral goodness.

Plato sees the harmonies of shape as not only characteristic of good culture but also characteristic of 'nature, animal and vegetable'. The symmetries of nature and the symmetries of art are in some intimate relationship with each other, as if there is in both man and nature an impelling function to seek form. Furthermore, Plato includes in his aesthetic education 'every kind of manufacture'. There is no divorce between art and manufacture, between aesthetics and practicalities. Good form is not only necessary for sculpture and art, but also for furniture, utensils, carpets, tools and machines - and the making of such objects is seen as an essential element of what Plato calls the 'true education of the inner being'.

Herbert Read in his book *Icon and Idea* contends that Plato's theory of art has been much misunderstood and misrepresented. To try and recreate the true nature of Plato's position he quotes R C Lodge, who in his *Plato's Theory of Art* argues that:

> The truly artistic life is not (as Plato sees it) a 'vita contemplativa'. It is not a life withdrawn from activity and concentrated upon perception or reflexion. It is the life which realizes in practice the ideals which it apprehends. The citizens of the model city are themselves the 'personae' of a drama which is, precisely, ideal community living. They live artistically. They project themselves into their roles. They make, each of them, an individual contribution to the integrated life of the whole. The general citizens, indeed, are living in a kind of dream-aura. They are all dreaming parts of one and the same dream. But their life is not a mere dream, forces of pleasure (as such), or wealth or power (as such). It is a dream which has a sense of guidance towards a final, ideal vision. This vision they are capable of apprehending (for the most part) only through art. They are helped by the music, the architecture, the marches and rituals which are an ever-present feature of their life.

There is, of course, an attraction in the unified culture which Plato depicts. But it is ultimately a false attraction. For all its strengths, Plato's philosophy of art is, ultimately, against life.

Plato, in order to secure harmonious culture in his Republic, edited the great myths, cut out chunks of Homer, banished tales in which gods behaved immorally, and exiled, with some remorse but with no uncertainty, the free poet. Only a simple and austere art, its content in agreement with the good, was allowed. In brief, only a closed ritualistic symbolism was permitted. Such symbolism has the power of engendering a great sense of unity and solidarity, but it can very soon stifle the creative quick, the spontaneous energies seeking new forms and meanings. According to Lodge, the members of the cultured community 'were all dreaming parts of one and the same dream. It is a dream which has a sense of guidance towards a final, ideal vision'. There may be an important place for a settled and comparatively closed symbolism, and particularly so in the education of the young. But unless this symbolism is complemented by another mode of symbolising which is personal and experiential, the society, and therefore the life of individuals within it, becomes frozen, confined to a set measure which can only be endlessly repeated. We need, in fact, to keep alive and vibrant two different elements in culture, one which is inherited and has something of the coherence Plato demanded, the other which is innovative, restless, seeking, even disruptive. They are in opposition but, like most opposites, they are in need of each other. Traditional culture provides the materials for innovative culture, but the two cultures gaze in opposite directions. Traditional culture is concerned with fidelity to the community and to the received traditions which make community possible. Innovative culture is concerned with fidelity to individual experience, that which is known, sensed, felt, apprehended from within. There must often be war between these two cultures, and, if a living balance is to be sustained, neither side must win.

Plato had no room for innovative culture, yet without it his own culture would have quickly become a matter of barren repetition and lifeless ritual. For this reason alone Plato's aesthetic theory is inadequate. Plato sees art as imitation, never as exploration. It is interesting also how having provided for the young such a broad education, he then insists on the severest specialisation. Indeed, for Plato, the artist in portraying the world was at a third remove from the source of truth. What the senses perceive, taste, smell, touch, hear, is always imperfect, a shadowy copy of something beyond. Truth, as embodied in the ideal forms prior to materialisation, archetypal and eternal, can only be reached through the operations of the unimpeded intellect. Above Plato's Academy was written 'A Credit in Mathematics Is Required', and one of his frequent remarks was 'God is always doing geometry'. In the end, what the senses and the feelings revealed were inferior parts of a dark realm, incapable of penetrating the real. The arts, on his own argument, constituted only a preparation for the higher life of reason. *The reason is the true self* - as with Descartes. Perhaps, then, it is not surprising with the Renaissance and the revival of Greek learning and scholarship, that *the cultural themes* of Plato and Aristotle were discarded as superfluous. Plato had elevated the mathematical reason to the top floor in the house of consciousness. It was to this top floor that the

Rationalists took their bags and scientific instruments. Why bother with second-order realities of culture, when the world was written in the clear and primary language of mathematics?

Throughout the analysis I have suggested the need for wholeness of being. I have criticised the dominant Western traditions of philosophy for excluding from their analysis the immense and rich complexity of actual experience. We are not pure minds, nor are we bundles of sense-perceptions. To insist that we are is to distort the nature of what is. Our experience is elusive, many-stranded, ever-changing, problematic, unfolding; it includes, often simultaneously, thought, feeling, imagination and sensation in one creative manifold. We are creative centres constructing a world we can inhabit out of a world which is terrifyingly dense and seemingly indifferent. Through the powers of symbolism, and particularly through the powers of language, we are able to grasp our own inner being and assert values, beliefs and aspirations. These are meaningful simply because they arise out of our existence in personal and endless attempts to clarify, to contain, to understand. The arts are valuable because they are an essential part of the existential quest for meaning, and because they keep sharp and subtle and various the tools necessary for the task.

Perhaps, wholeness of being is the ethical goal which all aesthetic activity moves towards, the artist desiring to confer on his own existence the unity he perceives in the best of his artefacts. Wholeness of being may have to remain, for the most part, a beckoning ideal, but if it is to be real and not counterfeit, it will have to include, in a tense balance, all the elements in the human psyche: thought, feelings, sensation, intuition, imagination and instinct. The arts, because they actively engage, in one way or another, all these elements, are best equipped to contribute to the development of such an ideal. The arts do, sometimes quite dangerously, enlist the magnificent monsters of the passions, but they also enlist the constructive, cognitive and form-seeking energies of the intellect. It is precisely because the arts, by their very nature, bring into free play the various and conflicting powers of the psyche and seek a living unity between them that they merit a decisive place in the curriculum.

I would like to conclude with a few practical reflections. I argued earlier that society needs two types of culture, one hereditary, communal and somewhat static (like Plato's), the other innovative, immediate, personal and dynamic, and that both had to engage with

42

each other, and that both, for the well-being of society, had to stand their ground. In our schools, alas, we have neither cultivated ritual and ceremony, nor individual exploration and creation.

The world 'initiation' has been recently used to denote the nature of the true educational process. It is a good word, but those who have used it in educational circles have robbed the word of some of its more potent connotations. We know from studies of primitive societies that initiation ceremonies are powerful, dramatic events in which the transformation of man from one level of being to another is demarcated and symbolised. Initiations are communal ceremonies with elaborate structures and powerful symbols. They mark important stages in the individual's life as it is seen by the community with all its complex and rotating needs. Dance, drama, singing, recitation, ritual are often all used to make palpable and real the transition from one stage of social existence to another.

In our own history the Reformation and Industrialism were together directly responsible for destroying many of these festivities and rituals. Susanne Langer in *Philosophy in a New Key* pointed to the general impoverishment of our symbolic environment. Reflecting on the work experiences of millions of people in factories (and, one might add, offices), she writes:

> This sort of activity is too poor, too empty for even the most ingenious mind to invest it with symbolic content. Work is no longer a sphere of ritual; so the nearest and surest source of mental satisfaction has dried up.

And, looking beyond work to our general condition, she concludes:

> All old symbols are gone, and thousands of average lives offer no new materials to a creative imagination. This, rather than physical want, is the starvation that threatens the modern worker, the tyranny of the machine. The withdrawal of all natural means for expressing the unity of personal life is a major cause of the distraction, irreligion and unrest that mark the proletariat of all countries. Technical progress is putting man's freedom of mind in jeopardy.

Schools alone cannot provide single answers to such enormous problems but they can develop ritualistic occasions, ceremonies which convey a sense of unfolding drama, a sense of a community giving symbolic form to its own deepest needs. The young are clearly attracted to football because it provides many ritualistic elements lacking in their lives. These ritualistic elements should be incorporated into the life of schools and refined and deepened. At the back of my mind I have two images. One is of the Welsh *Eisteddfodau,* beginning in the smallest villages and moving up to the national celebration, with singing, harp-playing and recitation. The other image is of a class of thirteen-year olds in a Steiner School giving a customary farewell to the single teacher who had taken them right through their primary education. I entered the hall quite by accident. It was dark because the curtains had been drawn. At the back a mass of candles on a large cake with many tiers were being lit. At the front, behind the curtains, there was the bustle of movement as the class prepared to make their various dramatic presentations to their teacher. And the hall itself was full of children, parents and teachers. The ceremony was expected to last a number of hours. In the new term the class would graduate to a higher level where they would be taught by many different teachers representing the specialised areas of human knowledge and an expanding adult community. What I had stumbled upon was an initiation ceremony, dramatic, ritualistic and communal.

These examples may seem far removed from urban life, television-culture, and our large examination-obsessed Comprehensive schools, yet in the nature of things children in any school have to move, at critical junctures, from one level to another. Perhaps teachers should develop ways not only of making these changes clear but also of making them the opportunities for symbolising, and thereby conferring a richness and depth to the shared rhythms of ordinary life? We need to develop, particularly in our drab secondary schools, a sense of ceremonial occasion. Perhaps, to make the suggestion a little more concrete, we need to introduce into each term a major festival exploring a major theme in which children and teachers collaboratively work on a programme of events. Such festivals might tap and draw upon the deep, symbolic needs of the human mind and provide the occasions for the community to experience its own power, its potential identity. Ceremonies could be developed in relationship to the natural cycle of Winter, Spring, Summer and Autumn, in relationship also to historical, local and religious events and occasions.

But such ceremonies, while necessary for the life of the community, are not sufficient: they need complementing by another mode of

44

symbolising, which is more personal and experiential. Here one of the aims of the teacher of the living arts is to promote among his pupils a fidelity to their own experience, whether actual or imaginative, and to all that slumbers within it. The most obvious characteristic of the arts is that they are stubbornly specific, not convertible into generalities, are imbued with all the qualities of their creators. 'The style is the man', said Flaubert, and we should add '*this* man and no other'. Art, at one level, is the elaboration of experience through symbolic form. This elaboration is no easy matter: it requires a discipline and methods as exacting, however different, as any demanded by the Sciences or Humanities. Above all, it requires a knowledge of technique and exemplar as well as a certain open paucity of mind, a willingness to suspend judgement, a readiness to live with fragments and submerged half-thoughts, a commitment to living with work-in-process. And this creative receptivity - 'negative capability', as Keats called it - requires a context of trust, in which mistakes can be made, explored and used for the true development of understanding. And it is this kind of personal understanding which should lie at the heart of education in any cultural democracy worthy of the name.

(1979)

CHAPTER FIVE

Aesthetic Education: A Manifesto

One of the major confusions in the teaching of the arts revolves around the word *aesthetic*. I believe it remains a crucial term for both the renewal and the unification of the arts in education, yet it is a term that is constantly misunderstood and even maligned. In some quarters the word 'aesthetic' has followed the same track as the word 'academic' and denotes a certain marginality and basic irrelevance; thus as certain matters can be dismissed as 'merely academic', so in a similar spirit they can be dismissed as being 'merely aesthetic'. In a recent article on the arts Dr Ken Robinson, who has done so much practically to promote the arts in education in the United Kingdom, could yet claim: 'The issues we are concerned with in promoting the arts in schools are not to do with some esoteric aesthetic cause but with the general nature and quality of school education as a whole'.

The sentence merits some closer examination. First of all, it demonstrates the notion of aesthetic as some vague and remote entity. (Yet quite why an *aesthetic cause* should be assumed to be *esoteric* is not explored.) Secondly, it indicates how a certain argument for the arts, reacting against the notion of *specific aesthetic meaning,* is forced toward a rather generalised and, indeed, imperialistic defence of the arts as some kind of alchemical agent transforming the whole curriculum. It is precisely this movement, from a defence of the actual individual nature of art experience to a diffuse pastoral moralism, which I think has eroded rather than strengthened the true place of the arts in education. After all, one could put forward comparable arguments for including Yoga, meditation, hymn singing, vegetarian cookery - or a thousand and one other such pursuits. Such a general, imperious position also blindly ignores the truth that any study done well requires 'quality' and engenders a sense of well-being and individual pleasure. This rhetoric of pious pastoralism in the arts debate has developed out of a refusal to acknowledge the power and the autonomy of the aesthetic and has one deep root in the Progressive tradition. It has been particularly influential in educational drama. Here, for example, is what Brian Way had to say in *Development through Drama:* 'We are concerned with developing people not drama (and certainly not theatre)'. In such a bald statement it is not difficult to see how the psychological is pitted against the aesthetic and the artistic. Way's book might have been better titled *The Death of Drama,* for that is what the position entailed and, to a considerable extent, brought about.

The failure in 'the growth' and 'general quality' argument derives from an inability to *differentiate the arts* from other disciplines in such a way that they are established as autonomous forms of inquiry, unique disciplines of understanding with distinctive traditions which must thereby remain essential to any balanced and coherent curriculum. The failure is a philosophical one, and the consequences have been severe. It is high time to make the *aesthetic cause* not esoteric, but open and clear; open and clear to ourselves, to our pupils and students, to parents, school governors, politicians, and the society at large.

The aesthetic is most adequately conceived as a particular mode of responding to and apprehending experience. Let me put forward the argument by analogy with the mind's power of deduction. Through the ability to reason the human mind is able to isolate, explore, and resolve certain aspects of its experience. Of course, we all use the deductive mode more often than we formally realise. In ordinary conversations the deductive is registered in requests for *definition* ('What do you mean by that word?'), by charges of *inconsistency* ('That doesn't follow', 'That's muddled'), as well as by recognition of *fit* ('That follows', 'Can't disagree with that'). Once it has been developed deductive analysis can become formidably powerful and, in some philosophers, an all but habitual disposition of the mind. The deductive is expressed through conceptual thinking, but it is systematically developed through the symbolic forms of logic, mathematics, dialectical and analytical philosophy. Now I want to suggest that, similarly, the aesthetic *is a mode of intelligence working not through concepts but through percepts,* the structural elements of sensory experience, and *that the arts are the symbolic forms for its disciplined elaboration and development.*

The aesthetic, far from being 'esoteric', is the most basic mode of human response. The tiny child, the newborn baby, begins to mediate its world aesthetically: through touch, taste, smell, sound, vision.

Nearly all the early shaping responses of human life are aesthetic in character, bringing, through pleasure, pain, or a diffuse sense of well-being, intimations of the nature of our common world. Long before we are rational beings, we are aesthetic beings; and we remain so, though often undeveloped and unsubtle, till ultimate insensibility defines the end of individual life. For death, in the precise words of Philip Larkin, administers '*the anaesthetic* from which none come round'.

The etymology of the word reveals that there is nothing perverse in our use of it to denote a fundamental sensuous mode of human response and interpretation. According to the *Oxford English Dictionary*, 'aesthetic' derives from the Greek word meaning '*through the senses*'. The definition runs as follows: 'of or pertaining to *aestheta* things perceptible by the senses, things material (as opposed to thinkable or immaterial) also perceptive, sharp in the senses'. Thus, consistent with its original denotations, the first use of the word *anaesthetic* in English in 1721 meant 'a defect of sensations as in Paralytic and blasted persons'. The three definitions are given as (1) *insensible*, (2) *unfeeling*, (3) *producing insensibility*. Similarly, other related words - *synaesthetic* (feeling with) and *kinaesthetic* (movement feeling) - record and depend upon the same matrix: of sense, of feeling, and of sensibility.

It is essential also that we perceive the contiguity between sensation and feeling, of sensory experience *and* sensibility. Again and again the practices of our language, the inherited conjunctions and the daily alliances of our speech, suggest the intimacy of this relationship. 'To keep in touch' is both to keep in contact and to remain close in feeling. To *touch* an object is to have a perceptual experience; *to be touched* by an event is to be emotionally moved by it. To have a *tactile* experience is to have a sensation in the finger-tips; to show *tact* is to exhibit an awareness of the feelings of others. The very word 'feel' embodies the conjunction; one can feel both *feelings* and *objects*, and indeed one can do both simultaneously. Our brief analysis discloses that the aesthetic involves both the perceptual and the affective. The education of aesthetic intelligence must, therefore, be concerned with the development of sensation and feeling into what is commonly called sensibility.

Thus, our argument has taken us from the remote and esoteric to the ordinary and the actual, from vague moralisms to a number of living and connected principles. The aesthetic denotes a mode of response inherent in human life which operates through the senses and the feelings and constitutes a form of intelligence comparable to, though different from, other forms of intelligence, such as the mode of logical deduction. If these propositions stand, it becomes clear that the aesthetic is a much broader category than that of the artistic; it includes all manner of simple sensuous experiences, from, say, the pleasure of tasting food to enjoying the breeze on one's face. But, at the same time, *the arts* depend on the aesthetic modality because they operate through it. The various arts comprise the differentiated symbolic forms of the aesthetic modality. The implications of such a position for the teaching of the arts and of the place of the arts in the curriculum of human understanding are many and complex; but before considering some of them I would like to give a few examples of the aesthetic at work in the making of art and in responses to it. I will allow the accounts to speak for themselves, for their relationship to my argument will, I hope, be self-evident.

The German film director Werner Herzog described a moment of profound artistic realisation in the making of a short documentary film as follows:

> I chose to work with a Swiss ski-jumper who did incredible things - jumping far past the limits which are considered possible without injury. Everything was working out well enough; the endless technical problems were solved; but still, for me, the film wasn't clear. Then one night the film crew, myself, and some others grabbed the skier, hoisted him on our shoulders and ran with him through the streets. His thigh was on my shoulder and I could feel the weight of him there. At that moment, the film suddenly came quite clear for me. And it came through the physical sensation. I feel everything about the films I make physically. I like to carry the reels around and feel their weight. When we are shooting I sometimes even like to touch the film itself.

Defining his relationship to a play he will subsequently produce Peter Brook has written:

> When I begin to work on a play, I start with a deep, formless hunch which is like a smell, a colour, a shadow. That's the basis of my job, my role - that's my preparation for rehearsals with any play I do. There's a formless hunch that is a relationship with my play.

49

Joseph Conrad in a preface of his short stories wrote that the story writer, the art maker:

> appeals to that part of your being which is not dependent on wisdom; to that in us which is a gift and not an acquisition... to our capacity for delight and wonder, to the sense of mystery surrounding our lives; to our sense of pity, and beauty, and pain; to the latent feeling of fellowship with all creation - and to the subtle but invincible conviction of solidarity that knits together the loneliness of innumerable hearts.

And he continued by defining his own artistic intentions:

> My task which I am trying to achieve is, by the power of the written word, to make you hear, to make you feel, to make you see. That - and no more, and it is everything. If I succeed, you shall find there according to your deserts: encouragement, consolation, fear, charm - all you demand - and, perhaps, also that glimpse of truth for which you have forgotten to ask.

If we consider these testimonies, we can see that the sensation is not valued as such but rather the *apprehension* which lies within it. The film director, Werner Herzog, grasps the idea of the whole film '*through* this physical sensation'. In the case of Peter Brook the 'formless hunch', like a smell, a colour, a shadow, provides eventually the key to the structure of the play. Joseph Conrad's account brings this out well. First he emphasises *sense experience* (' to make you hear', 'to make you see'), then *emotional experience* ('consolation, fear, charm'), and then, finally, '*that glimpse of truth* for which you have forgotten to ask'. The sight of art brings, we might say, insight; the perception of art engenders *being perceptive*. That difficult but indispensable word 'truth' belongs to art as much as it belongs to philosophy, religion, or the humanities.

The limitations of the still dominant vocabulary of the arts become clear at last. Notions of art as 'therapy', 'release', 'self-expression' fall away as misleading and trivialising acts of aesthetic intelligence, for it is the nature of such acts that they belong to an open and public realm. Other fashionable notions concerning the ideological determination of art by the fixed conditions of society also break down, because great art also expresses a transforming act of the mind and is able to generate new meanings and new possibilities. Art not only reflects, it also has the power to *create*, to make new, to make different, to extend in radical ways both perception and its artistic grammar. The language of pure subjectivity (developed most fully by the Progressivists) and the language of pure objectivity (often developed by the Marxists) fail to describe adequately the nature of both aesthetic intelligence and artistic creation. For us the artist - the significant artist - is best conceived as a perceptual philosopher, as one who seeks, through the symbolic ordering of his or her sensations, understanding into the nature of human experience. Rembrandt's late self-portraits are testimonies to precisely this; they manifest the energy of reflexive consciousness to discern meaning within the sensory play of colour, texture, mood, and spatial relationship. The aesthetic act is directed toward the apprehension of truth. In and through his paintings Rembrandt interrogates existence.

Such a view of the nature and value of art demands a more comprehensive definition of reason and intelligence. And there are many signs that precisely this redefining of discourse is now taking place. It informs the influential Gulbenkian Report *The Arts in Schools*. It is central to the recent educational writing of Howard Gardner. The philosopher David Best in his most recent book, *Feeling and Reason in the Arts,* writes: 'What is required is a coherent conception of mind, rationality and feeling which recognizes the inseparably cognitive character of emotional feelings and, in particular, those involved in the creation and appreciation of the arts'. To correct and complement *conceptual intelligence* we need the notion of *aesthetic intelligence,* we need to see both in terms of cognition of meaning and of a balanced psyche, though, one further argument has to be made, and it has been implicit in our argument from the start. It is to do with the *artistic structuring of the aesthetic modality*. It is to do with the place of tradition and technique in the creation and appreciation of the arts.

The arts have, then, one major source in the sensory modes of human experience; they develop out of what Robert Witkin in *The Intelligence of Feeling* called the sentient impulse. They are the expressions of our bodies, of the pulsing rhythm of the blood, of the inhalation and exhalation of breath , of the immediate delighting in sensations: in sounds, colours, textures, movements, perceptions. Of all the modes of intelligence that can be tabulated, the aesthetic seems the most primordial. Yet while the arts have this source in the biological, they also have another origin, namely, in the historic world

51

of culture and, more specifically, in the whole symbolic field of the particular arts discipline. As soon as we sing, make stories and narratives, dance, paint, we not only express and satisfy bodily rhythms, but we also enter into and depend upon what is symbolically available, on what has been done by previous practitioners, and on how much has been effectively transmitted. Art comes out of art, as mathematics comes out of mathematics. We improvise with and even extend artistic grammars, but we rarely invent them; they are 'there' in the culture, and it is in the transpersonal culture that art is both made and understood. The development of the sensory mode as a means of apprehending the nature of human experience depends upon the availability and range of these artistic grammars.

The point can be made by one example. When we now look at the 'child art' fostered by the educational Progressives during the twenties and thirties, we do *not* see the unique vision of the child, although the work is often artistically very fine; we see the impressive emulation of the art of the time, either of pre-Raphaelite book illustrations or Expressionism. The 'self-expression' of the children was modelled (consciously or unconsciously) on the conventions of the art that surrounded them; thus that vogue world 'self-expression' (defined by *Chambers 20th Century Dictionary* as 'the giving of expression to one's personality as in art') did much to distort the perception of what was actually taking place in the art room. A *unique vision* was not being created so much as *a living vision* of the dominant art of the period. For many teachers still holding on to Progressive theories this may seem an extremely negative and dismal interpretation. From the point of view of this essay it is, rather, a definitive judgement, an axiom describing how things *are* - for we live in historic cultures and not in self-enclosed bubbles of originality. This is not a negative and damning state of affairs but *potentially* a liberating judgement. What it suggests is that the innate aesthetic intelligence (like any other mode of intelligence) can be nurtured through an initiation into the forms of the symbolic discipline. It suggests that in the teaching of the arts we need, with the right sense of tact and timing, to introduce the artistic grammar of expression, the tools, techniques, and traditions of the art forms, and a vast range of achieved work which, taken together, represent the variety of truths the art form can 'tell' through aesthetic response. It suggests that the arts thrive best not in private cul-de-sacs but at the busy crossroads of symbolic life.

Many art-makers have explicitly expressed their debts to tradition. Writers constantly assert that they have found their own 'voice' through the voices of others. In her *Letter to a Poet* Virginia Woolf wrote to a young poet:

> Think of yourself rather as something much humbler and less spectacular, but to my mind far more interesting - a poet in whom live all the poets of the past, from whom all poets in time to come will spring. You have a touch of Chaucer in you, and something of Shakespeare; Dryden, Pope, Tennyson - to mention only the respectable among your ancestors - stir in your blood and sometimes move your pen a little to the right or to the left. *In short you are an immensely ancient, complex, and continuous character*, for which reason please treat yourself with respect and think twice before you dress up as Guy Fawkes and spring out upon timid old ladies at street corners, threatening death and demanding two-pence-halfpenny. (my italics)

This profound sense of a common symbolic order informed the whole of T S Eliot's work, as it also informs, to take a radically different background and example, the work of the Afro-Caribbean poet Derek Walcott. According to a recent review article, Walcott:

> ...was encouraged by two teachers and a library: 'It couldn't afford trash. I've often wondered what would have happened if I hadn't encountered Shakespeare, Dickens - all those Faber and Dent library books - and the poets. I would set out to imitate them: I'd do one like Auden, another like Dylan Thomas - it was an apprenticeship'.
>
> Walcott now teaches "creative writing" at Boston. He'd approve the inverted commas, believing that you can't teach poetry, only "the craft of verse..." His sense of poetry as a craft is connected to his passion for community and continuity. He believes in shared voices, "a guild of poets, a craft in the best sense practiced," and argues that the *modern* preoccupation with self can be reductive.

Walcott's notion of "a guild of poets, a craft in the best sense practiced" expresses a sense of apprenticeship, of emulation, of continuity and development in art-making which is necessary to any arts education, whatever the art form and whatever the age of the student.

Yet any analysis of the arts in British education and, no doubt, any analysis of the teaching of the arts in the United States, would tend to show that, with great and important exceptions, this initiation into the symbolic field has not taken place. In a recent lecture Gombrich, reflecting on his own contact with art teachers, wrote:

> When I once lectured to a teachers' training class I was firmly told in the discussion that no teacher must ever show what he personally likes since he must not influence the child. I was even told elsewhere that visits to art museums by school children were frowned upon by teachers, who alleged that the late Sir Herbert Read put freshness and originality above every other concern. But why allow oneself to be influenced by Herbert Read and not by Rembrandt? Why teach the child the words of our language but not the images of our tradition? None of us has discovered Rembrandt unaided; how can any growing mind find a point of entry into the cosmos of art without being given the opportunity?

Similarly, in educational drama there has been a positive dread of the theatre and the acquired conventions of dramatic expression, a virtual denial of any responsibility to the symbolic field. Even in theatre itself, outside of the schools, there has been a provincial modernism of spirit. As Jonathan Miller expressed it: 'There's a provincialism about the English *avant garde* that fails to see itself as part of an ancient tradition going back through Dante to Virgil'. A similar denial has characterised dance and, to a lesser extent, music; while English studies during the last three decades has tended to confine its attention to contemporary work with a distinctive bias toward the limited genre of social realism (and concentrated on thematic discussion rather than aesthetic engagement).

If we accept the idea of a common symbolic order, if we accept the idea of a discipline having a body of distinctive work and a range of conventions, if, furthermore, we accept that creative powers and aesthetic appreciation develop in continuous contact with the whole field of the art form, then it follows that one of the art teacher's major tasks is to take the student into 'the cosmos of art'. Strange as it may seem, in many quarters such a proposal smacks either of the revolutionary or the reactionary.

Above all, the position I am advocating requires a re-evaluation of our habitual interpretation of inherited culture as 'high', 'archaic', 'out-moded', 'bourgeois', 'irrelevant', and so on. It entails a much more constructive and practical view; namely, that the tradition (by which I mean *the sum total of past practices in a particular medium*) constitutes the field in which all the art, made both by the established artist and the student art maker, operates and that, therefore, any education in that art form must include a working knowledge and understanding of the field. It is not 'a return to tradition' so much as a return to the meaning of an arts discipline. To 'do' art is to activate the field. To talk of an initiation into the cosmos of art is, in truth, to talk of an initiation into the essence of our subject.

In some ways this essay amounts to a personal attempt to re-write the last chapter of Walter Pater's *The Renaissance*. In that short, curious, dislocating chapter Pater defined a concept of aesthetic experience which, along with other Pre-Raphaelite formulations, did much to erode its true value. In his beautifully cadenced prose Pater wrote:

It is with this movement, with the passage and dissolution of impressions, images, sensations, that analysis leaves off - that continual vanishing away, that strange, perpetual weaving and unweaving of ourselves... For our one chance lies in... getting as many pulsations as possible into the given time... For art comes to you professing frankly to give nothing but the highest quality to your moments as they pass, and simply for those moments' sake.

Unintentionally, it is a most ironic closure to a book celebrating the public and cultural achievement of the Renaissance. Life, artistic life, for the figures celebrated in Pater's book - Pico della Mirandola, Ficino, Leonardo da Vinci, Botticelli, Michelangelo - had been anything but a high solitary pulsation before the inevitable event of death. Yet in Pater's closing manifesto the whole of cultural life is "dwarfed to the narrow chamber of the individual mind", and the aesthetic experience is confined to solitary impressions, unstable, flickering, and inconstant. In Pater, in other words, *the aesthetic mode becomes locked in itself and becomes no longer an agent of understanding and transcendence*; it becomes no longer part of a collective symbolic order for it serves only fleeting impressions, making them not more *meaningful* but only more *intense*. Art as sensation.

55

The aesthetic as a flux of sensory moments doomed to extinction! How strange that a major book on the Renaissance should close on such a nihilistic note. And how much the book tells us about the intellectual current of late-nineteenth-century Europe and the coming privatisation of art in our own century.

Our collective understanding of the word 'aesthetic' is still bound to the writings of "the aesthetes", of the Pre-Raphaelites and the Bloomsbury group. In this essay I have tried to undo that knot. I have wanted to affirm a number of complementary propositions. I have tried to show that the aesthetic refers to a basic modality of human intelligence and that it is enhanced and developed through the symbolic forms of the arts; that the arts, at their most profound and typical, are formally *heuristic* in nature and not merely hedonistic, that they apprehend meanings and values vital to our individual and communal lives, and, finally, I have suggested that the arts, seen structurally, form vast symbolic orders which it is the task of arts teachers to transmit, keep alive, and relate to their students' own artistic endeavours. This conception of art moves us beyond the private and privatising world of cultivated sensations and out into open spaces of transpersonal struggle and transcendence. Such a view entails the end of Modernism and has the power to engender a more comprehensive aesthetic, with both a cultural and biological source, for our time. Some of our best contemporary architecture already embodies the change and invites us to participate in it. It now requires a corresponding expression within our educational system.

(1989)

* si. EUREKA!
encouraging the desire to find out

CHAPTER 6

A Conservationist Aesthetic for our Schools

At the present time we are witnessing in the arts a profound conservationism of mood and disposition. *Not* Conservatism, but conservationism. This conservationism can be seen most dramatically at work in the visual arts; it is recorded, for example, in the marked return to figurative, narrative and landscape painting. It is manifested in the sudden flowering of Post-Modernist architecture which, *at its best*, relates buildings to their historic and natural environments, to their communities, and to the inherited grammar of architectural forms.

A similar spirit can be observed in drama, dance, music, literature and even film (as it becomes aware of its own eventful history, its quickly evolving conventions and techniques, its own canon of great works). In all of the arts one senses a common desire to reanimate the many variegated traditions eclipsed by the dazzling glare of the Modernist movement. The art-maker, art-critic, art-teacher have become, in part, earnest ecologists, determined to save threatened symbolic forms from extinction. For like the ecologist they know these forms are necessary to the vitality of the whole culture. It is now widely assumed in the general arts debate that the greater the plurality of expressive forms the greater the chances of true creativity. No longer in the arts is it a question of manically asserting one's individual freedom, one's special uniqueness, one's startling originality; it has become more a question of establishing a continuous symbolic community, of returning to sources, of re-establishing vital connections to the historic past as well as to the natural order.

As this emerging conservationist aesthetic is a reaction to the extremes of Modernism, I want first to analyze, however sketchily, that movement. I want, then, to briefly consider some of the implications of my argument for the arts in education, with a particular eye to ecological and environmental issues.

At the outset I must stress that the developments outlined here are already in motion. A remarkable change in the structure of our sensibilities is taking place. It is recording itself most dramatically in the arts. My task is to name the informing conceptions, to delineate their implications, to think them through into fitting educational policies and better teaching methods. As I see it, the emerging conservationism is not only intent on reclaiming the neglected traditions of the past, it is also engaged with a philosophical conception of man and woman as intentional and symbolic beings within the manifold of nature. 'Culture', writes the philosophical biologist Mary Midgley, 'is the completion of instinct'. That is exactly the notion of conservationist aesthetics! Culture is the outgrowth, the articulate culmination of our biological nature and consequently reflects within its forms and rhythms the natural history of all things. Art-making, at root, is thus neither the distorting sublimation of libido (as Freud contended) nor is it a secondary but, rather, it is a primary and transformative energy of our own nature within Nature, an activity we delight in and need to engage in for a full realization of our creative species. What is involved here is a biological grounding of mental and symbolic activity. Too many philosophers from Plato onwards have put mind on the other side of nature, thus making it alien; and too many, especially in the Empiricist tradition, have rendered the arts a secondary and essentially a trivial pursuit. The biological grounding of symbolic life returns art to the order of nature and makes it fundamental.

The two central strands of the emerging conservationist aesthetic can be discerned powerfully at work in the best Post-Modernist (or, as Mordaunt Crook prefers to call it, Post-Functionalist) architecture. The following account, emphasizing both the historic and the ecological dimensions, brings this out well:

> Critical Regionalism necessarily involves a more directly dialectical relation with nature than the more abstract, formal traditions of modern avant-garde architecture allow. It is self-evident that the *tabula rasa* tendency of modernization favours the optimum use of earth-moving equipment... The bulldozing of an irregular topography into a flat site is clearly a technocratic gesture which aspires to a condition of absolute placelessness, whereas the terracing of the same site to receive the stepped form of a building is an engagement in the act of 'cultivating'

the site. It is possible to argue that in this last instance *the specific culture of the region - that is to say, its history in both a geological and agricultural sense - becomes inscribed into the form and realization of the work.* This inscription, which arises out of 'in-laying' the building into the site, has many levels of significance, for it has a capacity to embody in built form the prehistory of the place, its archeological past and its subsequent cultivation and transformation across time. Through this layering into the site the idiosyncrasies of place find their expression without falling into sentimentality.

Post-Functionalist architecture is architecture which honours memory and the specificity of culture and place. In clarifying his conceptions, the above writer refers to a conflict between what he characterizes as 'universal civilization' and 'autochthonous culture'. His concept of 'universal civilization', as abstract, rational, pure, is very close to our own concept of the dominant Modernist spirit which I described in the first three chapters and to which I would now like to turn. What, then, *was* Modernism?

As a general orientation of the European mind it can be understood best, perhaps, as the formal rejection of the past (both biological and cultural) as offering any substantial guidance to the living of life. It can be seen as simultaneously emerging from, and marking the end of, the Renaissance. Arguably, it reached its zenith at the beginning of our own century and has begun to disintegrate in our own lifetime. Descartes can be considered in his mode of philosophy, if not in the practice of his life, as the first Modernist. Sitting alone at his stove or fingering the wax on his desk, analyzing the unreliability of his own sense data, Descartes desired a complete illumination into the fundamental structure of things, with no guide, no previous model and no reference back to the accumulated traditions of thinking. His self-imposed and solitary task compelled him to disown, as a matter of his method, all historic culture as well as his own biological nature. In terms of time his programme entailed the virtual annihilation of the past tense. That orientation, expressed in innumerable philosophies and further empowered by the growth of science and technology, has remained the dominant orientation of Western Culture ever since. To be 'backward-looking' in our culture is, indeed, to commit a grievous crime against those two validating tenses: time present and time future.

Consider, for example, two of the influential formulations of our own century; Walter Gropius' 'start from zero' and Jean Paul Sartre's 'existence precedes essence' (further clarified by 'there is no human nature' and 'to begin with he (man) is nothing'). Both share the same premise: the individual must begin *ex nihilo,* with nothing behind him historically, and with nothing conferred biologically. Modernism always desired to start from the blank slate, the *tabula rasa,* the white sheet. The essential conceptual continuity between the French philosophers Descartes and Sartre is extraordinary and further testifies to the long intellectual span of Modernism. In fact, it is an immense irony that Modernism, in spite of the rhetoric, constitutes a tradition: a tradition to end all traditions.

Modernism in the arts came long after Descartes. Most critics agree that it was a development of Romanticism, establishing itself around the middle of the nineteenth century and reaching its peak in the first decades of the twentieth century. Jungen Habermas defines this immensely complex phenomenon as follows:

> In the course of the nineteenth century, there emerged out of this romantic spirit that radicalized consciousness of modernity which freed itself from all specific historical ties. This most recent Modernism simply makes an abstract opposition between tradition and the present; and we are, in a way, still the contemporaries of that kind of aesthetic modernity which first appeared in the midst of the nineteenth century. Since then, the distinguished mark of works which count as modern is 'the new' which will be overcome and made obsolete through the novelty of the next style.

Aesthetic modernity, then, is also built on the notion of a radical discontinuity, on a self-conscious disruption of time's three tenses. An authentically modern work had to be 'of the moment', had to arrive, as it were, certified as being uncorrupted by the influence of past art. As was argued in the opening chapter, the very term *avant-garde* (at the vanguard, leading the time) tells us a great deal about the characteristic disposition of Aesthetic Modernism.

Such a disposition had to lead, sooner or later, to outer symbolic depletion and inner psychic exhaustion. By the law of its own premises aesthetic Modernism was doomed to extinction. The obsession, in the fifty years between 1930 and 1980, with artistic revolution, with strident change, with endless experimentation (more and more dislocated from the enriching sources of the past) had to culminate in visual gimmickry, dependence on counterfeit commercial iconography and a self-fulfilling minimalism. There are many fallacies in Aesthetic Modernism but the most notable is that of *historicism* in Karl Popper's sense. As was argued earlier, this fallacy involved the substitution of illegitimate categories for the evaluation and understanding of art. Art came to be no longer judged by its intrinsic aesthetic qualities but by its overt relationship to 'modern time'. Thus critics asked of a painting: Was it an advance on the last style? Did it 'go beyond' the nineteenth century, beyond Cubism, beyond Fauvism, beyond Abstract Expressionism, beyond Pop or whatever the last movement was deemed to be? Was it 'relevant'? Did it encode a message for the age? But all of these questions demonstrate a by-passing of the essential primary question: the aesthetic power of the work in its own right, in its own rich field of execution and expression. They all reveal an obsession with the temporary moment.

During the 1970s a desperate cant filled a growing sense of emptiness; by the middle of the 1980s the game was up. The architecture changed, as did the painters being exhibited in the major public galleries. There was a return to figurative and narrative painting. The Pre-Raphaelites were exhibited at the Tate Gallery, followed by Edward Hopper, John Piper and Francis Bacon. The Hayward Gallery (that hideous temple to functional Modernism) showed the landscape and narrative paintings of Edwin Burra; the Barbican displayed the work of Gwen John and then the work of the Neo-Romantics. All that the spirit of Modernism had repressed and negated was being rediscovered. The importance of the past tense was reaffirmed, as were the value of place, locality, community, ritual, myth, natural materials, ornamentation, beauty, and the numinous. The extremities of Modernism had brought to birth a conservationist aesthetic.

How does this conservationist aesthetic relate to the teaching of the arts? To begin to answer this question, it is necessary to examine our key word 'aesthetic' and to relate it to the biological notion of mind referred to earlier. 'Aesthetic' is often taken to denote something akin to refined, exquisite, 'arty' and is tinged with connotations of indulgence, excess, decadence (it is as if the Pre-Raphaelites and the Bloomsbury group had together sealed the word in amber). This, however, is not the use of the word intended here. By aesthetic, in contrast, we denote a kind of bodily knowledge, *an apprehension of patterns through the power of sensibility,* especially as it is formally expressed and developed through all the arts. Our definition honours the etymological root of the word (the original Greek *aisthetika* means *things perceptible through the senses)* as it also sustains the philosophical import of the word developed by Kant. For Kant, aesthetic response entailed an act of sensuous contemplation in which *meanings* were disclosed. These meanings were perceptual in kind, as opposed to conceptual, but, nonetheless, ordered, moving and significant. Put more dynamically we could say that the aesthetic is one of the great modalities through which we symbolically discover and extend our nature.

Thus we find ourselves not only engaged with the biological grounding of mind, but also with a major expansion in our concept of intelligence and rationality. As Howard Gardner claimed in *Frames of Mind* (subtitled *The Theory of Multiple Intelligences)* the idea of the plural form of intelligence is an idea whose time has come. His argument that there are different modes of rationality, relatively autonomous and innate proclivities of the mind needing, from the cultural environment, continuous sustenance for their fulfilment, is close to our own. Here I am anxious to stress the nature and value of aesthetic intelligence. Aesthetic intelligence is perceptual intelligence; it is nurtured and articulated, principally, through the major arts disciplines. Artists, we might say, are perceptual philosophers. Such an insight is crucial to the conservationist aesthetic I am trying to map.

One implication of this aesthetic for the curriculum is obvious: the arts must be conceived as one community. The arts belong together for they all work through the aesthetic modality and are preoccupied with the patterns of experience, particularly sentient experience, as they are formally reflected in the diverse symbols of art. The arts belong generically together and should be granted the same importance in the curriculum as other 'intellectual communities', such as the humanities and the sciences. This is the first general educational proposition of a conservationist aesthetic.

The second proposition derives more from the *conservationist* element and concerns an aesthetic awareness of the tradition. This actual reclamation of the various and neglected traditions of art - this restoration of the past tense in order to secure the proper aesthetic continuum of time is now under way. It can be seen in dance, for example, where Janet Adshead has begun a historic and analytic study of dance forms, thus making possible a sense of history where there has been only a sense of the contemporary. Drawing her work into educational dance, Anna Carlyle has written about an expansion of dance education which would:

> include any kind of style of dance and an understanding of its form and purpose. Such an expansion frees dance from the confines of the contemporary. Here it has the potential to discover a new set of relationships and expressive possibilities within an historic continuum. Dance reconnects with its past and becomes potentially richer for the encounter.

What Anna Carlyle conceives of as the next development for dance is paradigmatic for most of the other arts. At the moment one can sense among many drama teachers a desire to connect with theatre, while English teachers cannot but be aware of the dynamic *Shakespeare in Schools Project* where Shakespeare is returning, in the most bodily and dramatic manner, to both primary and secondary classrooms. Indeed, even the traditional concepts of 'rhetoric' and 'poetics' are returning both to literary discourse and the practice of writing in the English lesson. These acts of conservation are all scattered signs of the new aesthetic. What, then, are the implications for the Visual Arts? In a critical paper published in *The Journal of Art and Design Education* in 1983 John Steers wrote:

> The greater part of the work of the art department is concerned with the production of art objects of one kind or another and little allowance is made for the development of critical awareness or an understanding of the cultural heritage of this country or of mankind as a whole. There is little obvious sequence in art education generally, or specifically in the secondary school. At every stage there is a tendency to ask pupils to start again at the beginning and to ignore previous hard won experience... (It is) a confused subject area generally lacking in direction and purpose.

The diagnosis reveals nearly all the critical symptoms of Aesthetic Modernism. For it was Modernism that insisted dogmatically that we 'start again at the beginning', from an impossible zero, from some assumed *tabula rasa* of the mind. Since 1983, though, there has been a formidable reaction against the 'tabula rasa classroom'. There has been a growing recognition that the child has to be brought into the visual culture, that he has to be made through the teaching of the arts a member of what Ernst Gombrich has called 'the cosmos of art'. In this context the principal publication has been Rod Taylor's pioneering work *Education for Art.* This book, first published in 1986 and illustrated by the remarkable work of young students who had often gone unnoticed in the *tabula rasa* art-room, sought to show that one of the responsibilities of the art-teacher was precisely to 'promote critical awareness', 'an understanding of the cultural heritage of this country' and 'of mankind as a whole'. Taylor's book shows how all four elements of the aesthetic field - making, presenting, responding and evaluating (drawing on the whole tradition) - can be brought in the right environment into a complex, interactive dance. The book can be seen to vindicate much of the theory and practice of a conservationist aesthetic.

This is not the place to demarcate the diverse genres of the visual arts. But it is of importance to my general ecological theme to consider further the renewal of interest in figurative and landscape art. Glancing over the rubble of International Modernism we find ourselves able to see, more clearly, certain continuities in British painting. As Peter Fuller has claimed:

> The best British artists have stubbornly maintained the traditions of an aesthetic rooted in the human figure and, indeed, in the imaginative and spiritual response to the whole world of natural form - including, of course, abstract forms derived from the experience of nature.

Thus it is possible to discern powerful connections between Henry Moore, Graham Sutherland, Paul Nash and the great landscape tradition of the late eighteenth and nineteenth centuries: of Palmer, Cotman, Constable, Turner. The painter Paul Nash, in particular, was quite emphatic about the aesthetic siting of his own lyrical painting (and photography). He referred to the 'English idiom of painting' and saw that idiom as using 'a pronounced linear method in design, no doubt traceable to sources in Celtic ornament or the predilection for the Gothic idiom'. Like so many of the landscape painters, his work is also central to our ecological understanding for it celebrates the fusion of imaginative consciousness and the organic structures of nature. It reveals a profound indwelling of mind within the order of nature.

Reflecting on this aspect of his work Herbert Read wrote:

> The natural organic fact, the present life of flower and leaf, invades the animistic landscape, the sacred habitation of familiar spirits. The shell, the fossil, the withered stalk, fungus, tree and cloud, are so many elements in a druidic ritual. The synthesis, the solution of the equation, is not literature: it is not metaphysics. It may be magic, but, if so, it is reviving the first and most potent function of art.

Read's commentary comes close to understanding but then confuses with its talk of 'magic' and 'druidic rituals'. It might have been better to say that Nash perceptually discloses the creative life of consciousness-within-things. In his work (as in so much of the British figurative and landscape tradition) we contemplate the patterning of nature as it is transformed through the imagination and the expressive qualities of paint. Nash's synthesis may be sacred but it is also, fundamentally, ecological - as, indeed, is the whole tradition to which the work belongs. I mention the British landscape genre partly because it is one of the traditions which should be brought into the art classroom, but also because, once again, it demonstrates the necessary continuum between past and present and between consciousness and nature.

There are two further facets of a conservationist aesthetic which, in conclusion, I would like to briefly consider. The first, relates to the use of natural materials. The second, to the teaching of design.

For obvious reasons a conservationist aesthetic would be committed, but not exclusively so, to the use of natural materials. Seonaid Robertson has shown the value of natural dyes in fabric work, but she has been even more eloquent about the aesthetic potentiality of natural clay. In a recent interview she claimed:

> Clay has the special nature of plasticity. It will take the imprint of the youngest child, or the most accomplished potter. It seems almost to take the emotional imprint of each person; one can look at a model in clay and see what state of mind the person was in. A visit to a museum, or even handling one humble clay pot the teacher has brought in, comes alive when we try to identify with the maker, see his thumbprint.

We can certainly show children that when they use clay they are part of a great tradition going back to the early history of mankind. Clay is the most indestructible of materials: when archaeologists dig into a site they often find the most information from pottery. And, looking forward to contemporary times, we can show children how great artists of today use clay for pottery and sculpture. Children can be led to feeling part of a living tradition. Clay is one of the important materials because of its wide location over the earth and its use from primitive times. I could teach every subject in the curriculum through clay.

In her spontaneous remarks nearly all the central points of a conservationist aesthetic are quietly reiterated; using clay, she affirms, children feel they are part of a long tradition. As their fingers and hands make connection with the malleable clay so the clay connects them both to the earth and the variegated cultural forms of the past.

Finally, with regards to design, a conservationist aesthetic would make two fundamental points. The first is that design should be conceived as a specialized development coming out of a more comprehensive visual arts aesthetic. Only this could ensure that the concept of design (which is of the greatest importance) would be informed by a developed sense of beauty and unity. The practical tasks would then be met with *aesthetic intelligence*. In this connection we must not forget how modernist architecture failed because of its *unremitting functionalism,* isolating the technical problems from the environment, from the community, from the actual places where the buildings were sited, from the whole web of connections which define the human-cultural-natural continuum of our lives. It would be a tragedy, if having recently freed ourselves from the functional and monotonous forms of Late Modernism, their discredited utile premises were to be laid down for a vocational 'arts education' in this country. Demands for 'training', for 'skills,' in relationship to 'market forces' disconnected from meaning and from ecological understanding, must have disastrous consequences. Design will only be good when it comes out of a full aesthetic education and is a manifestation of that aesthetic intelligence which perceives holistically and is able to execute accordingly. I have argued that culture is natural, that aesthetic activity is the way in which the mind makes perceptual sense of the world and that it is formally developed through the arts. I have tried to show how, reacting against the exhaustion of Modernism, a conservationist aesthetic is at work in our culture and in our educational system, transforming our practices and expectations. I have suggested that this conservationism of mood has brought the arts together as a unified community and has engendered a radical commitment to tradition (seen as part of the aesthetic field). In particular, I have wanted to make explicit the connections between the symbols of art, the aesthetic intelligence which creates them and the formative energies of nature through which our aesthetic intelligence has evolved.

(1988)

Autobiography as the quest for Individuation

For twenty years I have worked on and with autobiography; I have attempted to write it, to study its development as a literary genre and to use it in teaching as a technique to deepen the experience of learning. The first essay in this section offers a brief analysis of some fine autobiographies written in England during the last fifty years. The next essay introduces the great autobiography of Edmund Gosse *Father and Son* and develops a method of interpretation which moves between the conscious and unconscious intentions of the writing, a kind of psycho-analytical reading of autobiography. The three last pieces are much more personal. They reflect on my own attempts to create autobiography, and to use it in education; they also show how my own commitment to arts education derives from my own autobiography.

CHAPTER SEVEN

Quest for Identity: an Introduction to the Field of Autobiography

It is a sobering reflection that until about 1960, the year in which Roy Pascal's *Design and Truth in Autobiography* was published, there had been in Britain virtually no significant appraisal of the actual nature of autobiography. The somewhat earlier publication of H.N. Wethered's study *The Curious Art of Autobiography* (1956) illustrates the poverty of English analysis before this period. There, in the very opening sentences of the Foreword of the book, the author blankly states:

> This is a book about autobiographies. As a literary form these have passed through many phases in history and supplied us with many works combining considerable quaintness and much useful information.

Considerable quaintness:. much useful information. If these were the defining qualities of autobiography from St. Augustine to Rousseau, from Rousseau to Edwin Muir, their absence from humanist and literary studies would be amply justified. However, such superfluous observations reflect not on autobiography *per se* but upon the quality of the critical analysis and, beyond the individual study, to the general lack of any tradition in our culture for the evaluation of autobiography. For every hundred books published on the novel, there must be one on autobiography and, I believe, a definitive study of the form still remains to be written. Nevertheless, it would be entirely misleading to suggest that there are no important studies. Since Roy Pascal's book, the study of autobiography has shifted to America. In 1972 James Olney published his pioneering *Metaphors of Self: the Meaning of Autobiography* and in the years following that work there has been a steady flow of books from American scholars. Indeed by 1980 the tone of American critics in the study of autobiography had changed from that of strident proclamation to that of gentle apology. William Spengemann, for example, in his introduction to *The Forms of Autobiography* published in 1980 writes almost defensively:

> Had I written this introduction even five years ago, I could have begun, as was then the custom among critics of autobiography, by lamenting the scholarly neglect of this worthy literature. Now... the genre has become critically respectable, not to say fashionable.

Alas, what has been firmly established in America has only just begun to take root in our own culture. American pop culture has an infinitely greater velocity than that of American criticism and scholarship.

However, the lack of an adequate theory of autobiography has not inhibited the writing of autobiography. Quite simply, autobiography thrives. Writers write autobiography. Readers read it. Publishers publish it. Libraries stock it. Is it that in an age which so ubiquitously threatens our sense of personal meaning, we become preoccupied with the question of identity and, consciously or unconsciously, turn to autobiography to see how others have managed to secure their sense of a self, hoping, also, that from their struggles we may find clues to our own uneasy quest for identity? I think there is considerable truth in such a reflection. Certainly autobiography, at its best, is engaged with ontological questions, with true and false modes of being in the world. Virginia Woolf in her fragment of autobiography *A Sketch of the Past* establishes some of the necessary terms when she refers to 'moments of being' and 'moments of non-being' and claims that the moments of non-being prevail. Part of the task of autobiography is to locate those moments of being in which the self, as it were, coincides with self and intuitively recognizes an existential rightness and an underlying pattern. Herbert Read in the Preface to the 1962 edition of his autobiography, *The Innocent Eye*, claimed that to establish one's individuality (in the writing of autobiography) was possibly the only effective protest against what he saw as the permeating power of the collective death wish. Perhaps, then, we as readers turn to autobiography for the images and narratives of struggling existence, wanting to contemplate the hidden forms of inwardness, wanting to discover the concealed springs of life. Whatever the interpretation, the fact remains that the genre thrives. It is not easy to get a precise figure for autobiography alone, but at the present time over 1,300 new biographies and autobiographies are published in Britain every year. The following list will give the reader some indication of the extent to which writers use the form. It is not intended as a definitive list; it begins with Virginia Woolf and closes with Richard Hoggart, who published his autobiography *A Sort of Clowning* in 1990.

VIRGINIA WOOLF, *A Sketch of the Past* (written 1939-40). ENID STARKIE, *A Lady's Child* (1941). ELIZABETH BOWEN, *Seven Winters* (1943). OSBERT SITWELL, *Left Hand, Right Hand* (1945). JACK CLEMO, *Confessions of a Rebel* (1949). SEAN O'CASEY, *I Knock at the Door: Swift Glances Back at Things that Made Me* (1949). ARTHUR KOESTLER, *Arrow in the Blue* (1952). STEPHEN SPENDER, *World Within World* (1953). EDWIN MUIR, *An Autobiography* (1954). C.S. LEWIS, *Surprised by Joy* (1955). RICHARD CHURCH, *Over the Bridge* (1955). DAVID DAICHES, *Two Worlds: an Edinburgh Jewish Childhood* (1956). JAMES KIRKUP, *An Only Child* (1957). LEONARD WOOLF, *Sowing* (1960). CECIL DAY-LEWIS, *The Buried Day* (1960). JANET HITCHMAN, *The King of the Barbareens* (1960). FRANK O'CONNOR, *An Only Child* (1961). J.B. PRIESTLEY, *Margin Released* (1962). HERBERT READ, *The Contrary Experience* (1963). RONALD DUNCAN, *All Men are Islands* (1964). P.J. KAVANAGH, *The Perfect Stranger* (1966). V.S. PRITCHETT, *A Cab at the Door* (1968). STORM JAMESON, *Journey from the North*, Volumes I and II (1969 and 1970). DANNIE ABSE, *Ash on a Young Man's Sleeve* (1971). LOIS LANG-SIMS, *A Time to be Born* (1971). GRAHAM GREENE, *A Sort of Life* (1971). MALCOLM MUGGERIDGE, *Chronicles of Wasted Time*, Volume I (1972). KATHLEEN RAINE, *Farewell Happy Fields* (1973). WINIFRED FOLEY, *A Child in the Forest* (1974). COLIN MIDDLETON MURRY, *One Hand Clapping* (1975). CHARLES HANNAM, *Boy in Your Situation* (1977). EDWARD BLISHEN, *Sorry Dad* (1978). JOHN OSBORNE, *A Better Class of Person* (1981). PATRICK WHITE, *Flaws in the Glass: A Self Portrait* (1981). JANET FRAME, *An Angel at My Table* (1984). ANN OAKLEY, *Taking it Like a Woman* (1984). RONALD FRASER, *In Search of a Past* (1984). PETER FULLER, *Marches Past* (1986). ARTHUR MILLER, *Timebends: A Life* (1987). ANTHONY BURGESS *Little Wilson and Big God* (1987). GERMAINE GREER, *Daddy, We Hardly Knew You* (1989). JOHN UPDIKE, *Self-Consciousness* (1989). RICHARD HOGGART, *A Sort of Clowning* (1990).

Of course, such a list only represents a tiny fraction of autobiographies published during the last five decades. It does not include the innumerable autobiographies written by those who have distinguished themselves in other fields: by composers, artists, dancers, singers, politicians, philosophers, industrialists, academics, film stars, journalists, pop-stars, media pundits etc. Nor does it include obvious autobiographical novels (like Raymond Williams' *Border Country*, 1960, or David Holbrook's *A Play of Passion*, 1978) nor all those cultural studies with an essential autobiographical base (like Richard Hoggart's *The Uses of Literacy*, 1957, or those made by the Oral History Society). Yet for all the wealth of material, for all the abundance of published life-stories, it must be frankly admitted that while nearly all are of some general human interest, only a few possess the artistic power and the depth of good imaginative literature. Too many autobiographers evade the full challenge of the form: they elect to shape only the external elements. The temptation is to establish a public portrait which, ultimately, exists to flatter both author and reader.

The problem with many English autobiographers is that they refuse to break the national vice of protective reticence and social urbanity. One of the great strengths of Lois Lang-Sims' *A Time to be Born* is that it is prepared to shock the reader with the almost inhuman intensity of the hatred for her mother, even when her mother is dying. Social form demands that such feeling is repressed: but good autobiography must express it, especially when it is crucial to the full understanding of the author's experience. (Anthony Rossiter's *The Pendulum* and Jack Clemo's *Confessions of a Rebel* have the same quality of an all but explosive emotional honesty.)

In the autobiographical act it may not always be clear what the position of the reader is. In reading an autobiography he finds himself being more than a passive spectator. Quickly, even reluctantly, he becomes implicated. He is addressed sometimes as sympathetic witness, sometimes as objective judge. Frequently, he is appealed to as independent listener. The reader, it could be argued, is the objective 'other' which makes the autobiographer's confession a reality and not an act of solipsistic introversion.

An analysis of the historical development of autobiography confirms such a concept of its nature. The word 'autobiography' was first employed in 1809 - at the height of the Romantic period - and the first formal use of the word 'autobiography' in publishing was in 1834 when W.P. Scargill's volume *The Autobiography of a Dissenting Minister* was printed. But the form of autobiography goes back through fourteen centuries to St Augustine's *Confessions* written in the second half of the fourth century. These words 'autobiography' and 'confessions' - and the particular historical tides on which they bob - are charged with meanings which we must not overlook. The Confessions of the Christian period can be viewed, from one perspective, as the sacrament of confession metamorphosed into literary form; the Autobiographies of the Romantic and Modern periods can thus be understood as those Confessions secularized. In their transformed state acknowledgement (confession derives from the latin: *confiteri*, to acknowledge) of past failures is made first to the self (not God) and then to the reader (not priest). Confessions, in their traditional form, crave forgiveness; autobiography desires understanding. Confessions are devoted to salvation; autobiographies to individuation.

As with the sacrament of confession so with St Augustine's *Confessions*; it begins with a prayer taken from the tradition, 'Can any praise be worthy of the Lord's Majesty? How magnificent his strength! How inscrutable his wisdom!' The author submits himself to tradition. His opening invocation taken from the Psalms is one of many forming a persistent thread in the tapestry of the writing. He addresses his self-analysis not to himself or to the reader, but directly to God:

> My soul is like a house, small for you to enter, but I pray you to enlarge it. It is in ruins, but I ask you to remake it.

The work is a passionate examination and recreation of the author's past before his Maker and Judge; the motivating force comes from the desire for inner renewal. As in the sacrament of confession, the failings of the past are brought consciously to mind in the present for the securing of the future - the quintessential autobiographical rhythm.

Although there were many significant movements in the development of self-reflection and self-recreation between St Augustine and the eighteenth century - in the writings of, for example, Petrarch and Montaigne, or, to take a closely related medium, in the self-portraits of Rembrandt (who all but obsessively recorded himself at every significant stage of his own life) and Dürer (who with a new found audacity painted himself in the image of Christ) - it is yet commonly accepted that it was Rousseau who was to take the form of autobiography dramatically further, or, more precisely, to give it its modern shape. His *Confessions* is a great and original work sounding a new key:

> I have resolved on an enterprise which has no precedent, and

75

which, once complete, will have no imitator. My purpose is to display to my kind a portrait in every way true to nature, and the man I shall portray will be myself.
Simply myself.

Here lies the character of true *auto*biography, its characteristic mood and predisposition. The writing describes the unfolding life of the unique self (*auto-bios-graphein*). And does so without apology. Even if in the third paragraph there is, as in the confessional manner, reference to 'my Sovereign Judge', the tone is gently mocking and the author - staying firmly at the centre of the stage - retains authority. In Rousseau we find the traditional confessional style transposed into a new key, that of autobiography as a quest for self-definition and for authenticity of being.

After Rousseau the autobiographer addressed himself directly and had for his listener, not priest or congregation, but the individual reader. The new context, the evolving form, the formation of a more precise word placing the burden on identity, manifested (as did the parallel emergence of the novel) a deepening concern for psychological truth, for the infinitely subtle processes of individuation rather than the definitive once-and-for-all matter of salvation. The number of writers employing autobiography after Rousseau - Goethe, Wordsworth, Herzen, Mill, Ruskin, Tolstoy, Gorky, Gosse, Darwin, Newman - demonstrate that the form had come of age. Our own century and our own times continues to testify to its indispensable place in the act of self-exploration and actualization. As Ronald Duncan put it, in the first sentence of his own autobiography, *All Men are Islands*: 'We settle down to write our life when we no longer know how to live it.' During a period of tremendous confusion in beliefs and values we have evolved autobiography to secure some sense of order and inner identity.

It is not possible to embark upon a lengthy evaluation of three of the more remarkable autobiographies published in our century: Herbert Read's *The Contrary Experience*, Kathleen Raine's trilogy beginning with *Farewell Happy Fields* and Edwin Muir's *An Autobiography*. But I bring them together because in literary style and guiding predisposition they seem to me to stand together. They possess the same literary strengths - they are all remarkably eloquent testaments - and they raise simultaneously a cluster of awkward questions about identity and authentic being.

'Perhaps the best autobiography in our language.' So claimed Graham Greene of Herbert Read's *The Innocent Eye* and, initially, one is tempted only to modify that judgement to '*one* of the best'. It is incomparably the best section of *The Contrary Experience*, a volume made up of four discrete autobiographies written at different times and under different circumstances and brought together as late as 1962. *The Innocent Eye* is a precise poetic re-creation of Read's childhood memories of his father's farm. There are twelve sections each named after a particular place or object, e.g. the Vale, the Green, the Orchard, the Cow Pasture, the Church, the Mill, and each section concentrates on the memories which the place elicits. The book begins with the birth of the writer and ends with the death of his father. The object of the last section is explicitly titled 'Death' and refers also to the death of the child's vision, the termination of his visionary world.

The work has the classical formality of a Baroque concerto. It is free of sentiment. As there is no self-consciousness in the memories, so there is no self-consciousness in the writing. Like Wordsworth's *Prelude*, with which it has much in common, it presents the experience of immediate vision, the 'thereness' and 'thatness' of the child's unpremedidated consciousness, yet paradoxically caught in a language quite beyond the range of the child: the first person singular is used most sparingly for the *objects* perceived and recreated through the autobiographer's memory define his nature. Where the innocent I is the innocent eye, vision is identity. For Herbert Read such experience is definitive:

> All life is an echo of our first sensations, and we build up our consciousness, our whole mental life, by variations and combinations of these elementary sensations. But it is more complicated than that, for the senses apprehend not only colours and tones and shapes, but also patterns and atmospheres, and our first discovery of these determines the larger patterns and subtler atmosphere for all our subsequent existence.

All the bright moments of ecstasy derive, Read insists, from 'this lost realm'. We progress only to repeat, with less resonance, what has already been given.

But the great bulk of *Contrary Experience* is made up of three other volumes (*The Innocent Eye* comprises only forty pages of a substantial volume). These volumes simply do not possess the same extraordinary power of verbal enactment of the first volume. From a literary point of view, *The Contrary Experience* moves from highly condensed expression to conceptual generalization; moves from metaphor to abstraction; from poetic embodiment to the mere tinkle of 'ideas'. Is it possible that the literary failure is a direct consequence of the informing concept of self which is seen, as it moves away from childhood, to enter exile and unreality? Does the failure of the work to develop cumulatively through time expose a prior failure in a conception of identity which cannot move through time from childhood without diminution? Is it farewell to those happy fields of which, at best, one can only ever capture a dying echo?

The first volume of Kathleen Raine's trilogy, *Farewell Happy Fields*, recreates her childhood and adolescence; the second volume, *The Land Unknown*, describes her experience as a student at Cambridge University in the thirties, her two short-lived marriages and her various reactions to Positivism, Marxism and Catholicism, all of which she partially embraced only to disown as distorting commitments, distracting her from her own authentic vocation. The third volume *The Lion's Mouth*, is largely and courageously confined - although that is quite the wrong choice of verb for such a volcanic experience - to the author's attachment to Gavin Maxwell. Of the three volumes *Farewell Happy Fields* is the masterpiece, a sustained piece of autobiographical recreation on a par with *The Innocent Eye*. The language is simultaneously lyrical and precise; it is able to embody the most elusive and haunting of childhood memories:

A little hand of flame, blue tipped, thin, labile, without substance or constant form, dancing gently on a gas-jet from the wall. In my warm cot gently laid to sleep I watched those luminous fingers dancing for me, for me. I found a song to rise and fall with the hand of the flame, glimmer and glum, glimmer and glum, glimmer and glum, and so on and on. The living flame was a being, strange and familiar, familiar and strange. My father would turn it out, send the little hand away.

The rhythms there convey exquisitely the mesmerized moment in which object, self and symbol flow together only to disappear out of the stream of consciousness. Kathleen Raine also, but much less frequently, captures the moment of childhood trauma which has its root in the child's spontaneous identification with the world. In the following passage she narrates the death of the bull:

> There was a long waiting; the butcher, alone, crossing the yard, gun in hand; a muffled blow, and as in a Greek tragedy the king is slain behind the heavy doors of his palace, so we waited for the shot, and knew that the great one of our small world, the creature of power, had once again been slaughtered; the strong by the weak, the great by the small. Presently, as from those palace doors, the great body was dragged out of the byre and on to the dray, limp and powerless. I saw his pepper-and-salt purplish-brown hide with a sense of infinite compassion: I *was* him. My body suffered in itself the death of the beast, my skin mourning for his skin, my veins for his veins, my five senses for his; and when from that anus slipped a mass of faeces, I was ashamed for the abasement of his death.

The death of the bull is presented as the death of a god. This, too, is characteristic of Kathleen Raine's instinctive approach. The isolated event is taken down into its deep archetypal structure and so made universal. Thus simple places are converted into spiritual conditions - Ilford becomes Hades, Scotland becomes Paradise, London a kind of Purgatory ('but now, in London, in order to survive at all, I must simulate some other person, or perish') - and her journey becomes, at best, the journey of Everyman. Her life becomes her 'story'; her story becomes her 'myth'; her myth, in as much as myth is always representative, becomes that of our own experience. No sooner does she name an object than it becomes a symbol of the imaginative life. And it is here that one is able to identify both the great poetic strength and the possible existential failing of the trilogy. When the myth-making propensities of her imagination are converting childhood memories into living symbolism - when the childhood experiences recalled are meeting the needs of the present and leading to transformation and renewal - one feels the essential rhythm of good autobiography. But when she takes her later experience, experience in which she seems unable to encounter 'the other' even as it gives birth to vision, we find ourselves, as readers, perplexed. We cannot help asking: is the vision attained at the expense of self-knowledge? Is the mythic narrative at the expense of the psychological? Does this numinous world of the imagination depend upon the dissolution of the full impinging actuality of many diverse worlds which nevertheless come together in any one experience? Does the predisposition to see self as child-like visionary innocence inevitably lead to a trilogy which begins with a literary masterpiece (where childhood is evoked) and yet which, in spite of all its honesty and passion, fails to culminate in any comprehensive significance? Is the author's concept of self adequate to the full task of autobiography?

In Edwin Muir's *An Autobiography* there is a greater sense of growth; there is repetition and return, certainly; but there is also development and integration. The first part, *The Story of the Fable*, was published in 1940 and then incorporated into the complete autobiography first brought out in 1954. The autobiography takes us in chronological order through Muir's childhood in the Orkneys, his experience as an adolescent and young man in Glasgow and Fairport; it narrates his activities and relationships as an emerging writer, in London, Prague, Dresden, Helleran, Italy, Austria, France, Prague again (this time under a Communist regime), and lastly in Rome where his commitment to Christianity finally crystallizes. The places are important because they mark the stations of an inner journey. Rather like Ilford in Kathleen Raine's *Farewell Happy Fields*, so Fairport (where Muir works in a bone factory of unbelievable squalor) represents the negation of all positives. In Virginia Woolf's terms Fairport symbolizes Non-Being - and in its hideous machinery Muir is tragically entangled for many years. The Orkneys symbolize a prior Eden before Fairport. The two visits to Prague, in part, represent two versions of politics, the liberal and the totalitarian, the open and the closed. While, at one level, the reflection takes the reader deep into archetypal structures - into 'the fable' and those moments of being 'liberated from the order of time' - it is open, at another level, to the fact of historical and biological process, of relationship and social obligation. Individual being is seen as the reel on which the radically different strands of life are wound. There is both a sense of exile (therefore a movement backwards) and a sense of indivisible unfolding (with a forward motion) and such a dialectic allows for individual growth and pain and anguish.

The opening chapter of *An Autobiography*, describing Orkney, has a visionary intensity. The reader is gently taken through a sequence of vast still-life images, of childhood memories which have become primordial. The incidents remembered have become so slowed down they imperceptibly slip into a kind of eternity. The power of the writing depends on paragraphs rather than sentences but the following account, describing his father sowing seeds in the spring is characteristic:

> I would sit watching him, my eyes caught now and then by some ship passing so slowly against the black hills that it seemed to be stationary, though when my attention returned to it again I saw with wonder that it had moved. The sun shone, the black field glittered, my father strode on, his arms slowly swinging, the fan-shaped cast of grain gleamed as it fell and fell again; the row of meal coloured sacks stood like squat monuments in the field.

These childhood images were later to form the primary material of Muir's poetry:

> A little island was not too big for a child to see in it an image of life; land and sea and sky, good and evil, happiness and grief, life and death discovered themselves to me there; and the landscape was so simple that it made these things simple too.

Yet it is a measure of Muir's growth as a poet and as a man that he is able to employ the childhood images to convey not the world of a child but the hidden import of the most catastrophic events of our era (as, for example, in his great poem *The Horses*). Muir's imagination is as capable of presenting the experience of unreality and nausea as of glory and innocence. His chapters on Glasgow and Fairport are so disturbing to read for they recreate, in the way that Herbert Read's War Diary in the *Contrary Experience* fails to, the weird phenomena of dislocation and psychic disease. In fact, Muir has an all but frightening ability to define with a poetic precision the lineaments of pure emotional states. He is the William Blake of autobiography.

His comprehension of depth and complexity is further recorded in his attention to dreams. Should the autobiographer present the streaming images of the unconscious as well as the events and circumstances of everyday experience? Muir writes:

> It is clear... that no autobiography can confine itself to conscious life and that sleep, in which we pass a third of our existence, is a mode of experience, and our dreams a part of reality. In themselves our conscious lives may not be particularly

interesting. But what we are not and can never be, our fable, seems to me inconceivably interesting.

For this reason Muir describes many dreams in his autobiography, but surface and underground are not forced to inhabit the same level; they are allowed to co-exist. The fable is not the life; mythic time is not historic time. These very distinctions make possible a development and comprehensiveness missing in the other autobiographies. Yet, they in turn create their problems. For where is the self which would mediate between the diverse and distinguished worlds? And how can the nature of that self be known when many of its truths are out of reach, for much of the time, in the darkness of the unconscious? There are only fragments, memories, elusive movements and 'in a great number of dreams... a few glints of immortality'.

To consider the three autobiographies together is to detect certain similarities. The writers belong to the same generation; they are poets; they have deep roots not in the urban but in the rural order; they suffer exile; they leave their social class and background; they devote their lives, in different ways, to the truths of the imagination. In their autobiographies, at least in their most memorable and haunting sequences, one becomes aware of the common quality of the language which, while it remains wholly contemporary, still has behind it the gravity and grandeur of the Authorized Bible and the sinew and pulse of Shakespeare. They also have that unusual power to lift ordinary experience up into the symbolic dimension where it is given an enduring significance, where it becomes, in Muir's phrase, part of the fable. At the same time, they present the reader with concepts of self which require the most delicate scrutiny. In the case of Herbert Read and Kathleen Raine we find the image of the visionary child which lies deep in the Romantic tradition, yet can the child ever act as metaphor for comprehensive existence? I have suggested that the comparative failure of their work to accumulate, to grow, to deepen, indicates not, in the first place, a literary failure, but a partiality of conception which derives from an inability to fully integrate the human dialectic and the appalling complexity of existence. In Edwin Muir's autobiography we find a similar commitment to what he called the child's 'original vision of the world'. But, at the same time, there is an authoritative recognition of its opposite state; a tacit appreciation of the role of negative experience in the ecology of consciousness. Hence

An Autobiography has a forward motion. The book develops as the author develops.

The problem which Muir's work raises relates to his persistent sense of the elusiveness and uncertainty of identity. The central preoccupation of autobiography with realization of self is cast into doubt. Perhaps identity is only ever a partial fragment of something larger and, forever, unknowable? Muir states emphatically: 'I can never know myself.' We are always and forever more than we can symbolically grasp. Such a view could be taken to define the limitations of the form. Alternatively, it could be seen as a further challenge to the dominant convention in autobiography in its use of the chronological and historical narrative. Is it not possible to write an autobiography which captures the truth of experience, with its uncertainties, gaps, aspirations, visions and banalities, without relying on the method of linear chronology? Does this hint at the next development in autobiographical recreation? If so, Muir's autobiography, with its sense of human life camped precariously on the border between the ordinary and the fabulous takes us, at points, very close to the new ground. Muir, at any rate, leaves us with the sense that self-knowledge must serve something other than itself. In this deep insight, autobiography, once again, finds its ontological source; moves us deftly from the certainty of knowledge into the mystery of being.

(1983)

CHAPTER EIGHT

Autobiography as Individuation:
the Strange Case of Edmund Gosse

Edmund Gosse's *Father and Son* was first published anonymously in the autumn of 1907. Although some of the initial reactions expressed a sense of alarm at what was discerned as a lack of filial respect the book was, for the most part, well received and before Gosse's death in 1928 was widely regarded as a minor classic. Indeed, within twelve months of its first publication there had been four further editions of the work and Edmund Gosse, habitually cautious and preoccupied with his own literary standing, was soon ready to shed his anonymity.

It is significant that *Father and Son* was more warmly received in the United States of America (where it was published in the same year), for in America the concern for propriety was so much less than in England and the Victorian division between the public and private realm was less tightly drawn, more open to negotiation between author and his reading public. It was not considered an offence to 'speak out' or improper to reveal the inevitable tensions between generations as they manifest themselves in family relationships in, for example, the prolonged and not always conscious struggle between vulnerable, resistant sons and invulnerable and powerful fathers. In a private letter dated 2 February 1908 the American Shakespearean scholar, Howard Furness, had written to Gosse:

> At two sittings I read every word of it. It is a very great book. The best you have written and the most enduring; with it you will celebrate your century. English literature cannot afford to let such a book die. Independently of its record of a rapidly vanishing faith it is told with an evident truth as unflinching as it is tender.

Furness' remarks were, no doubt, more accurate than he had intended for *Father and Son* was to be the only book of Gosse's to survive the sudden eclipse of his prodigious reputation which followed upon his death. But the immediate recognition of the work is clearly recorded in his response, as it is in another letter sent to Gosse on 16 January 1910 by the American novelist William Howells:

> I read slowly and faithfully and I have got only to the point of your mother's death. But what a world I have passed through! There is a universal truth to child life in it all, and the specialized truth is most wonderful and pitiful. I have fairly ached along the story. In all the autobiographical books I have read I remember nothing equalling it.

In a further letter, written five days later, Howells confirmed the truth of his first reactions, praised the diction of the book as 'exquisite in its tender precision' and, with not uncharacteristic American euphoria, claimed:

> The pathetic tale could not be better worded if a syndicate of masters rose from their graves to do it; say Milton, Dante and Shakespeare. Truly a most beautiful book.

Gosse never received quite such adulation from his English critics but the reputation of the book grew steadily in this country and its achievement was widely acknowledged. George Bernard Shaw declared it to be 'one of the immortal pages in English literature' and even the young and pugnacious Ezra Pound, in a destructive review of Gosse as representative of official and otiose British culture, yet conceded: 'Gosse has written one excellent book: *Father and Son*.' In 1927, a year before the death of Gosse at the age of seventy-nine, Harold Nicholson also drew attention to the book, naming it 'a masterpiece' in which 'the author had been able to combine the maximum of scientific interest with the maximum of literary form'. We will consider this judgement at a later point but whatever its critical value it further buttressed the reputation of the book. For as the years passed and as Gosse's vast opus of essays, sketches, poems, plays and biographies turned yellow and gathered layers of library dust *Father and Son* remained in print and found, generation after generation, an appreciative audience of readers. As Furness had said, it was the best Gosse had written and the most enduring.

It is somewhat difficult for us now living in the latter frayed part of the twentieth century, where private lives are ready material for instant public consumption, to envisage the kind of courage Gosse required to write the work and why, until the fourth impression of the book, he chose to publish under the protection of anonymity. Harold Nicolson in *The Development of English Biography*, declaring that Victorianism only died in 1921, referred to 'the shock' occasioned by the publication of *Father and Son*. Even Evan Charteris in his biography (1931) of Edmund Gosse hints at the degree of the alarm by the kind of defence he proffers:

> Those who take the view that *Father and Son* disregards reticence and respect will see... what forbearance Gosse exercised and how much he has toned down in that book... Few have kept the fifth commandment so closely.

Such a commendation is made only when considerable doubt has been cast upon the matter. (And yet, tellingly, the statement itself is unintentionally ambiguous; if the author has 'toned down' his true feelings then, perhaps, indeed he had not inwardly honoured his parents.) For the time in which it was written *Father and Son* was a courageous work although, as we shall see, its courage was frequently inhibited by countervailing pressures which forced the existential truth to work often under the surface of the text and even against its ostensible and scientifically described aims. Yet in its struggle to confront family relationships descriptively rather than rhetorically; in its attempt (though impeded) to delineate honestly the tensions between father and son; in its partial desire to offer a portrait of an eminent Victorian in terms of human fallibility and, indeed, gullibility; in its unexpected and, perhaps, unintended concluding manifesto announcing the right of the individual 'to fashion his inner life for himself' even against the dictates of tradition and parental values, and certainly against the injunctions of puritanical patriarchs, in all of these things *Father and Son* was a somewhat subversive work for those capable of discerning its full implications.

Edmund Gosse wrote in a perceptive review of Lytton Strachey's *Eminent Victorians*, one of the next major works in non-fiction to break away from the tradition of eulogy and rhetoric in the description of individual life:

> Their (Victorian biographers) fault lay, not in their praise, which was much of it deserved, but in their deliberate attempt in the interests of what was Nice and Proper - gods of the Victorian

Age - to conceal what any conventional person might think not quite becoming. There were to be no shadows in the picture, no stains or rugosities on the smooth bust of rosy wax.

Gosse titled his evaluation of *Eminent Victorians* 'The Agony of the Victorian Age'. Agony is a strong word, particularly so for Gosse, and it is one that does not frequently appear in his writings. He meant it. The agony of the Victorians resided in the schizoid split between public and private, between the large formal gesture and the intimate personal actuality. It expressed itself at every level of Victorian life and seemed at its most hypocritical in the area of sexuality. For Lytton Strachey the contradiction manifested itself dramatically in the literary form of biography where Victorian biographers privately knew one thing about the eminent figures they portrayed and publicly wrote another. Although Gosse cautiously welcomed *Eminent Victorians* and later in 1927 dedicated his last book, *Leaves and Fruit*, to its author 'with affectionate admiration', he too was a Victorian living out 'the agony' of a divided consciousness.

To give one example, Gosse wrote the life of Algernon Charles Swinburne (published in 1917) but, at the same time, compiled a *Confidential Paper on Swinburne's Moral Irregularities*. He must have felt that the official life could not fully impinge upon the complex actuality of the man; there was public knowledge and there was private knowledge and even in the delicate interpretive act of critical biography discretion kept them apart.

Gosse's ambivalence, his conflicting desire to preserve social decorum and yet seek existential truth, provide us with a key to unlock his own autobiography. In *Father and Son* we sense an unresolved war between compliance and authenticity. This struggle lies not only at the centre of his childhood and adolescence, but also (though less obviously) in the very style and organization of the book. Reading the book one occasionally senses in a phrase, a sequence of sentences, even a whole paragraph, a complexity of contorted emotion of which, one suspects, the author himself was largely unconscious. For Gosse reveals more than he ever proposes in his analytical introduction. To fully comprehend the text and to be able to place it both within and beyond its historical context, the reader has to be prepared to live simultaneously with at least two versions of the work. The first version is the consciously determined one, written with sufficient respect for the Victorian Gods of Niceness, Propriety - and one must quickly add a third - Objective Science.

The second version has a different dynamic; it spontaneously emerges at points only to be repressed - to function at deep unconscious levels in the verbal organization of the work - until it finally manifests itself in powerful, unambiguous terms in the closing Epilogue. The first version is ironic, detached, scientific, neutral, urbane, sociological. It has great biographical and historical value. The second is exposed, passionate, labile, inward and deep. It has the power to move and disturb. It has true poetic and autobiographical energy. The first version is written from the wary Victorian intelligence; it has a shrewd eye to the audience, a concern for tact and decorum, and has come to believe, like Darwin and Spencer, in the pure objectivity of Science. The second version is the unsettling subjective voice of the more honest but dispossessed modern, of authenticity struggling outside communal values and inherited judgements, ready, at least in principle, to fashion its own inner life. But this is to anticipate later analysis...

That *Father and Son* in its style and narrative records both the Victorian and the modern sensibility goes some way to account for the enduring importance of the volume. And yet little had been written about the book. It has received little sustained critical interpretation. It has been not exactly ignored, for it has been given many passing references in literary and historical writings, but nor has it been closely examined. Its wealth of ambiguity, of contradiction, its seesaw dialectic between conscious intention and actual revelation has not been fully delineated or its significance demonstrated. There have been a few perceptive forays, of which Virginia Woolf's spiky essay 'Edmund Gosse' in Volume IV of her *Collected Essays*, and David Gryll's brilliantly probing analysis in *Guardians and Angels*, are by far the best. Many essays, like V S Pritchett's in *The Living Novel*, are merely anecdotal; others inertly descriptive. There is a similar paucity of material on the man. Osbert Sitwell's account of Edmund Gosse is slight, self-advertising and 'literary'. James Woolf's study, *Sir Edmund Gosse*, while giving some information, is devoid of intelligence. The main source for biographical material remains Evan Charteris' *The Life and Letters of Sir Edmund Gosse*, published in 1931, although there is a well-documented account of Gosse's lecture trip to America in 1884 and of his literary relationship with that country in *Transatlantic Dialogue: Selected American Correspondence of*

Edmund Gosse. In brief, the materials are sparse and any systematic interpretation of the man or the *opus* virtually non-existent, though Ann Thwaite's recent rather unadventurous biography has altered the situation a little. Given the success of *Father and Son* during the length of this century, this is an oddity which calls for some explanation.

Part of the reason must lie in the eclipse of Edmund Gosse's reputation. In 1920 Gosse was one of the most influential figures in English cosmopolitan literary life, at the heart of a complex web of relationships which included Henry James, Thomas Hardy and André Gide. By 1940 he was all but forgotten. If his poetry or criticism had possessed the power of Coleridge's or Arnold's, doubtless his autobiography would, as a consequence, have received close critical attention. However, his poetry rarely transcended the sticky mannerisms of the Pre-Raphaelites and his criticism, while comprehensive in range and lucid in style, tended to be limited by the superficial approach of belle-lettrism. The titles of the books, *Some Diversions of a Man of Letters, Critical Kit-Kats* and *Gossip in a Library*, convey the inveterate disposition of the armchair critic. The words 'charming', 'entertaining', 'exquisite', 'tasteful', 'adorned', litter the pages and tend to obscure any more probing insight which, at times, is seriously at work. We must not forget that Gosse found in literature a refuge from the chilling demands of his puritanical background - *Father and Son* is, in large measure, the record of that momentous personal discovery - and that, for this very reason, he was somewhat reluctant to be deeply disturbed by it or, in turn, to be disturbing in his judgements of it. In the light of his background, it is not surprising to find in personal correspondence, if not in public disclosure, that Gosse hated 'the cocaine and morphine' of Dostoyevsky, that he could not tolerate Tolstoy as social prophet and disturber of the status quo, and that E M Forster's *Howards End* outraged him for 'introducing into fiction a high-born maiden who has had a baby'. He called the book 'sensational and dirty and affected'. Against this, however, must be recorded his early recognition of such major writers as Ibsen, Whitman and Gide.

The weakness of Gosse lay in his aestheticism. Charteris says that Gosse believed: 'If the reaction to a literary work was pleasure, they had an adequate basis for criticism without any sizing up of moral values'. But this hedonistic approach to literature floundered badly as civilization encountered the irrational slaughter of the First World War; it had no way of engaging with the upheaval because aestheticism itself was ultimately more a symptom of the malaise than interpretation or corrective. In the changing conditions, Edmund Gosse's lightness of touch became not so much sensitivity as a lack of pressure; the super-refinement, in the crisis of civilization, became a mode of superficiality. As the critics, F R Leavis, Ezra Pound and T S Eliot made in the struggle for standards and meanings a trenchant stand against the Pre-Raphaelites, Gosse's voice grew thinner and thinner until it became a disappearing whisper. One work remained: *Father and Son*; and because it was solitary it missed the scrutiny it merited.

There is, though, a further reason for the critical neglect of *Father and Son*. It relates to the genre. Autobiography has, until recently, eluded serious study. We have innumerable works on poetry, on drama and the novel but only a handful of books inquiring into the distinct form of autobiography. There can be little doubt that *Father and Son* has suffered as a result of the failure to establish in our culture a critical method and a fitting discourse for autobiographical writing. It is time now to make a closer examination of the work.

In a symposium of essays, *Approaches to Victorian Autobiography*, Phyllis Grosskurth claims:

> The typical Victorian autobiographer was acutely aware of his audience. A mutual complicity shaped the genre, and language became a screen to shelter the vulnerable egos of writers and readers alike.

As we examine *Father and Son* (published only a few years after the Victorian period had technically closed) we will need to bear this judgement in mind; we will, at times, need to lift the language screen to see what inner drama lies behind it, what emotions it is consciously or unconsciously intended to conceal. It is vital to our understanding of the book to comprehend the conditions in which Victorian autobiography (and biography) was expected to function.

In editing a version of Count Carlo Gozzi's autobiography during the Victorian period, John Addington Symonds decided to expunge 'those passages and phrases which might have caused offence to some of my readers'. Edmund Gosse himself in a review of a new translation of Montaigne's essays (essays which in their own way formed during the early Renaissance a magnificent assertion of autobiographical understanding) wrote:

> Montaigne, living in an age when speech was free, frequently touches upon subjects of delicacy. He is never morbid or offensive, but he is sometimes outspoken. At such moments, without any emphasis, Mr Ives simply allows his author to retain his own native speech until he ceases to be indiscreet. No method could be more praiseworthy.

The implication is that the Victorian age is not free; subjects of delicacy have to be veiled. We constantly stumble across a sense of restriction in the matter of personal communication. Of Walter Pater, Gosse writes 'his faith [in the human race] was never positive, nor would he trust it to read his secret thoughts'. Herbert Spencer in his *Autobiography* asserted simply that it would 'be out of taste to address the public as though it consisted of personal friends'. While Anthony Trollope, in his autobiographical account of his life and work published in 1883, cautioned: 'That I or any man should tell everything of himself I hold to be impossible. Who could endure to own the doing of a mean thing?' As for intimate relationships: 'My marriage was like the marriage of other people and of no special interest to any one except my wife and me.' Any intrusion into private space was considered indiscreet and, ideally, the private should conform to the public expectation, to the virtuous and heroic and productive. In the Victorian period, autobiography, developed to a pitch of inwardness by Rousseau, became the medium for masked truths and guarded reflections. Indeed, autobiography was in danger of becoming more external memoir than the exposed exploration and recreation of the elusive self.

Edmund Gosse's *Father and Son*, like its counterparts, Mill's *Autobiography* (1873) and Mark Rutherford's *Autobiography* (1881), is not written directly in the tradition of Rousseau or the earlier style of St Augustine. It belongs to its own age and country. Like a well-trained Englishman, Gosse has only to assert himself and he apologizes. If he proclaims, then he qualifies the proclamation out of existence. If he uncharacteristically expresses a powerful feeling he seeks immediately the first escape route he can find: all very English and, in particular, the inveterate disposition of the Victorian mind.

91

In her short study of Edmund Gosse, Virginia Woolf wrote perceptively:

> Fear always seems to dog his footsteps. He dips his fingers with astonishing agility and speed into character, but if he finds something hot or gets hold of something large, he drops it and withdraws with the agility of a scalded cat... We know all that can be known by someone who is always a little afraid of being found out.
> But if Gosse's masterpiece and his portraits suffer from his inner regard for caution, much of the fault must be laid upon his age.

Virginia Woolf defines the lack in the text and then places the text in context; the author does not only influence the public, the same public that he writes for can deeply influence him not only in what he presents but in how he does it. But, in a sense, contrary to Virginia Woolf's judgement, the reader, particularly from another age, can know more than the author intends, can detect what he may be unwilling to tell, can read the private underground of the text as well as the polite public surface, and can find the autobiography within the autobiography. Before we embark on such analysis I must first establish that the work *is* autobiography, for the claim has been challenged and, moreover, in the last chapter of *Father and Son*, Gosse himself denied it.

In *The Development of English Biography*, Harold Nicolson claimed:

> The book is not... a conventional biography; still less is it an autobiography. It is something entirely original; it is triumphant experiment in a new formula; it is a clinical examination of states of mind over a detached and limited period.

One can, of course, see what Nicolson means. Both the title of the book and the subtitle, 'A study of two temperaments', would seem to substantiate the judgement that the book is not biography or autobiography, but an experimental form combining both. In his own Preface Gosse states that the work is a *document* diagnosing Puritanism and a *study* of intellectual and moral development. More, then, a formal documentary, than an intimate autobiography? (Doesn't Gosse himself call it 'a slice of life'?) This view is not to be dismissed, for the historical value of the text lies precisely in this realm. We will examine this conception of the book later. I wish first to show that the book is significantly more than this and that its inherent shape and inspiration is, in fact, that of autobiography.

First, we have the evidence that Charteris provides concerning its genesis. According to Charteris, Gosse decided to write *Father and Son* at the suggestion of George Moore, a literary friend. Moore, having read Edmund Gosse's conventional biography of his father, urged him to rewrite the story, but making the conflict between father and son central. Apparently, he pressed this notion of another work many times, but Edmund Gosse did not respond with animation until Moore suggested he should adopt the first person singular, the autobiographical mode *par excellence*. Such a work should not, Moore insisted, be based upon factual records but upon the recall of his own memory, it was to be the son's view and it was to span the critical period between birth and his arrival in London at the age of sixteen. Once Gosse had perceived a personal and direct way of handling the material, he worked intensively and had completed *Father and Son* within a year. In short, the generative impulse was an autobiographical one; the first person singular was the key to the writing of the book.

Secondly, and as importantly, the text itself reads predominantly as autobiography. It is true that the book claims to offer us a study of two temperaments, but that study is not dispassionate and is always given from the son's perspective. The father we see is the father the son sees. We never experience any of the conflict from *inside* the father's position. He remains a more or less static figure who is judged according to the son's categories. The son, in contrast, grows continuously until he finds and defends his own emancipation. At the front of the book Gosse placed his epigraph: *Der Glaube ist wie die Liebe; er lasst sich nicht erzwingen*: 'Faith is like love: it does not let itself be forced.' That epigraph is not disinterested and impartial. It embodies, as the whole book does, the son's judgement of the father; it is the inexorable conclusion that the autobiographical narrative imposes.

There is, as Nicolson contends, an important historical and biographical element in *Father and Son*. There is a kind of objectivity. There are claims for scientific exactitude. It is also true that Gosse himself disowns the autobiographical form. And yet, without a doubt, the central story we are given is that of the son, from his birth to the point of his departure from the family at sixteen. And the son is the writer of the book. Such a narrative can only be called autobiography. Now let us turn to the work itself.

> At the present hour, when fiction takes forms so ingenious and so specious, it is perhaps necessary to say that the following narrative, in all its parts, and so far as the <u>punctilious attention</u> of the writer has been able to keep it so, is <u>scrupulously true</u>.

So opens the Preface to *Father and Son*. The insistence on clinical observation and exactitude runs like a steel girder through the Introduction. The word 'document' is italicized and is followed quickly by the words 'record' and 'diagnosis'. The reader is presented with the image of the writer as naturalist conscientiously noting all the details of the particular specimen and setting it against the background of the environment. The author-scientist is determined not to have his perceptions corrupted by sentimental feelings or the possible bias of self-admiration or self-pity. Indeed, in the first edition of the book the Preface draws attention to the author's anonymity:

> As regards the anonymous writer himself, whether the reader does or does not recognize an old acquaintance, met with in quite other fields, is a matter of no importance. Here no effort has been made to conceal or identify.

The work, it is insisted, is quite other than that of his 'other fields', his poetry and literary appreciation. (But the dogmatic assertiveness of the text fails to smother an obvious dilemma. Why, if there is 'no effort to conceal or identify' is the book published, in the first instance, anonymously?)

The first paragraphs of Chapter 1 continue in the same detached manner; it is as if the author is looking down on the two protagonists from a high vantage point, quite forgetting that he himself is one of them:

> Of the two human beings here described... There came a time... The struggle began soon. But to familiarize my readers with the condition of the two persons... and with the outlines of their temperaments... it is needful to open with some account...

<u>The method,</u> then, is that of <u>objective description</u>. The writer works within the paradigm of the inductive sciences. One can see why Harold

Nicolson concluded that the book was not conventional biography and still less autobiography. There are explanations for Gosse's intentions. There is, for example, the literary influence of the French critic Sainte-Beuve about whom Gosse said 'I am the disciple of one man and of one man only - Sainte-Beuve. No one else has been my master.' Sainte-Beuve had demanded that the critic should work as 'a good naturalist in the vast domain of the human spirit in order to classify the different orders and species of the human mind.' Sainte-Beuve had also talked of the 'unbridgeable² differences between intellectual types, differences of blood, of temperament'.

In these two notions of critic as naturalist and of the innate temperaments of individuals forming different species to be understood and classified, we can detect powerful influences on the formal construction and underlying conception of *Father and Son*. The notion of science must have been particularly attractive to Gosse for, by the end of the nineteenth century, many were claiming with increasing success that science was the sole way in which to arrive at any certainty in matters of truth. A commonsense inductive approach to life was beginning to prevail; arguments were to be resolved by reference to evidence and facts. As a study of the father *Father and Son* is, in part, the analysis of a man who could not, because of the power of 'the turbid volume of superstition', recognize the truth of the evidence under his very finger tips. The father 'took one step in the service of truth, and then he drew back in an agony, and accepted the servitude of error'. What is missing in *Father and Son*, however, is any conscious recognition of different realms of meaning; thus the scientific is seen as true and the inductive approach adopted as the method of the book. Such a method allowed the author, seemingly in good faith, to exclude the full emotional detonation of the narrative. In a diagnosis and a record one keeps subjective elements under control. Thus Gosse found a way of appealing to the three main prejudices of his time: a desire for decorum and for tact in private and emotional matters coupled with an inordinate belief in the power of the fact and the promise of progress.

As a documentary record we know, from other sources, that most of the facts are accurate. In the manner of a scrupulous biographer Gosse drew on all the accounts he could gather. He drew on the intimate diaries of his mother; on letters his father had written him; on an account entitled *A Memorial of the Last Days on Earth of*

Emily Gosse which his father had circulated after her death. Furthermore, Gosse had already published in 1890 a long formal biography of his father *The Life of Philip Henry Gosse, FRS* and therefore had a wealth of documented material to hand. We can discern the conscious approach of *Father and Son*: it is to be the work of a literary naturalist reconstructing, detail by detail, scrupulous fact by scrupulous fact, the social milieu and then to plot within it the forms of individual and innate behaviour. The impartial reconstruction requires that the author hold back any unruly squads of feeling and any imperious judgements of the heart. For this reason - at least at a conscious level - Gosse seems determined to be fair-minded, ready to qualify his own position, prepared to be judicious in the smallest matters. He also stands back from himself. In many of the early childhood memories, we sense the superior adult inspecting the folly of the once-child:

> My theological misdeeds culminated, however, in an act so puerile and preposterous that I should not venture to record it if it did not throw some glimmerings of light on the subject which I have proposed to myself in writing these pages.

'Puerile', 'preposterous'; the words suggest that the adult would hardly sink to consider the misdeeds were it not for the scientific urge to record all relevant facts. One would hardly think in such passages that the author had once been that very child. The quite remarkable experiment in worship is dismissed as 'this ridiculous act'.

The neutrality and remoteness which Gosse establishes in the Preface as the condition for the inquiry ensures a fidelity to outer detail, to encompassing context, to the actual chronological sequence of events. It gives the book an historical value. It paints in miniature a sharply drawn portrait of an age; it presents for our edification the behaviour of a provincial middle-class Puritan family; it conveys, above all, a sense of the traumatic scientific and religious ferment of the mid nineteenth century. (Darwin's *Origin of Species* was published in 1859.) Anyone wishing to understand the psychological and theological dynamics of that upheaval could not go to a more valuable account than that given in Chapter V of *Father and Son*. Yet, if this was all the book offered, it would not be the classic it is. There is another energy in the writing which is not accounted for in Gosse's clinical Preface. Indeed, so crucial is this energy to the full under-

96

standing of the work that we are led to ask whether, in fact, the Preface is one of those linguistic screens referred to by Phyllis Grosskurth behind which writer and reader alike could shelter their vulnerable egos. Is the Preface a kind of defence against the half-hidden existential meaning of the book, a defence of which Gosse himself was strangely unaware? This question takes us into a deeper reading of the text.

Although Gosse's style glides rather than penetrates, although it has a subtle propensity to skirt round and out of disconcerting experiences, although it easily digresses and qualifies, yet occasionally the reader confronts an emotion which is presented without defence. Of the death of his mother when the son is only seven, Gosse writes:

We had no cosy talk; often she was too weak to do more than pat my hand: her loud and almost constant cough terrified and harassed me. I felt, as I stood awkwardly and shyly, by her high bed, that I had shrunken into a very small and insignificant figure, that she was floating out of my reach, that all things, but I knew not what nor how, were coming to an end. She herself was not herself; her head that used to be held so erect, now rolled or sank upon the pillow; the sparkle was all extinguished from those bright, dear eyes. I could not understand it; I meditated long, long upon it all in my infantile darkness, in the garret, or in the little slip of a cold room where my bed was now placed; and a great, blind anger against I knew not what awakened in my soul.

This is a most moving autobiographical evocation of pure feeling; everything about the inner experience is caught: the feeling of smallness, of loneliness, of desolation, of emptiness, of anger. It is rendered subjectivity, without the mask of irony, without the pretensions of scientific documentation. And it is this kind of subjectivity running underground through the text, erupting at unexpected points and explosively in the Epilogue, which calls for a second reading of the work. What we must try to do is to locate the unintended but latent significance of the narrative even where it contradicts the conscious and manifest intentions of the autobiographer.

In a typical passage at the opening of a paragraph in Chapter IX Gosse morally praises his father:

97

My father was very generous. He used to magnify any little effort that I made with stammering tongue... The whole thing, however, was artificial and was part of his restless inability to let well alone.

Manifestly the intention is to honour the father, as would be expected by the audience, but the actual outcome is to negate the generosity. If it was 'artificial' and part of his inability to let well alone, in what lay the generosity? The high rhetoric of biography is used and quietly emptied of significance. Grylls, who has made the most perceptive study of *Father and Son* and who has analysed many of these curious contortions in which the manifest meaning is contradicted by the latent, writes:

His appraisals are expressed with civility and wit; he favours for his occasional strictures a tone of mild expostulation. And yet... here and there we sense something more intense; a discrepancy of judgement, a telling lapse of tone, a hint that not everything about his past has been so successfully subdued. We sense, surviving over the years, an animus against the father.

The force of the autobiographical and subjective experience rises up and works somewhat subversively against the scientific intentions of the work. Feelings do not have the unambiguous and static nature of facts. Or, to put it another way, there are no 'facts' in family relationships which are not made up of the deep and dialectical flow of feelings, exposed, irrational, multi-layered and labile.

Let us take another example. In the Epilogue Gosse defensively declares that his father was 'no fanatical monomaniac' and then, only a few pages later, insists that the allegation he has dogmatically rejected, is, precisely, the one which best fits. Considering his father's position, he writes with a directness which marks the Epilogue and isolates it from the main text:

There is something horrible, if we will bring ourselves to face it, *in the fanaticism* that can do nothing with this pathetic and fugitive existence of ours but treat it as if it were the uncomfortable ante-chamber to a palace which no one has explored and of the plan of which we know absolutely nothing.

His father is not fanatical on one page but is so, by implication, on

98

another (and indeed further back in the text, his volume *Omphalos* is dubbed as 'fanatical'). Such contradictions in the author make strange 'facts' indeed, facts which disclose more than the son, no doubt, ever intended.

At the beginning of the Epilogue Edmund Gosse's intention, once again, seems transparently clear:

> This narrative, however, must not be allowed to close with the son in the foreground of the piece. If it has a value, that value consists in what light it may contrive to throw upon the unique and noble figure of my father.

But does he execute what he promises? Once again, no. Not only in the very same paragraph is the father's nobility negated by the references to his psychological cruelty (keeping 'his Biblical bearing rein... incessantly busy') but, even more shockingly, the Epilogue concentrates on the son's response and ends triumphantly with his manifesto of emancipation:

> No compromise, it is seen, was offered; no proposal of a truce would have been acceptable. It was a case of 'Everything or Nothing'; and thus desperately challenged, the young man's conscience threw off once for all the yoke of his 'dedication', and as respectfully as he could, without parade or remonstrance, he took a human being's privilege to fashion his inner life for himself.

The manifest intention of the work is to end with the Victorian panegyric to the eminent patriarch: unique and noble. At this critical and falsifying moment in the book the unconscious thrust of the whole volume broke through the surface and made itself dramatically visible. The deeper purpose of the book was to justify the son's act of freedom. I also suspect that the emotional ambivalence was so great in Gosse that he failed to notice the shocking contradiction between the first and the last paragraph of the Epilogue. Yet, emotionally, dynamically, autobiographically, it is the necessary and moving culmination of the book. Our second reading of the text places the author's conscious intentions to one side and claims that the book is not primarily a study of two temperaments with an inductive approach to knowledge, but rather that it is the autobiographical account of how one of those temperaments, following the innate tendencies of its own nature, frees itself from submission to the other.

Such a definition of the main, if buried, purposes of the work, suggests a further but related way of interpreting the text. It can be read, as many other autobiographies, as a quest for individuation. *Father and Son* shows, perhaps more consistently than anything else, those stages of inner growth which make possible the eventual emancipation from the all-encompassing puritanical environment. 'Certain leading features in each human soul are inherent to it and cannot be accounted for by suggestion or training,' Gosse maintains. Thus the son discovers his distinct sense of identity through a cumulative series of incidents which bring a sense of self coinciding with self and the experience of 'rapture'.

These incidents *happen*. They are not engineered; they have no place in the planned environment, though they implicitly hold within them the promise of the future. The book is full of such resonant moments: the very early response to Uncle E. and to the smell of tobacco, the discovery of the two selves in the garden, the reading of the sensational novel in the attic, the witnessing of Punch and Judy, the first awed response to the sea, the listening to his father's reading of Virgil, the discovery of *Tom Cringle's Log*, the reading of the funereal poets in the garden, the exposure to *The Tempest*, the buying of the poetry books, the violent attraction to the pagan statues. All of these moments confirm, enhance and extend the son's sense of self. Against this emergent, if highly vulnerable sense of self, operated the organized pressures of the Puritan environment and the indomitable will power of his father. The struggle is, then, that between authenticity and compliance. Edmund Gosse moves uneasily between the two; now adapting to the dictates of the father; now responding, with lyrical delight, to the surfacing elements of his own nature; now cunningly adopting the mask of 'unctuous conformity' to secure his own ends; now losing his own identity completely in the external environment. From this perspective, the book is about the struggle of the self, in a hostile environment, to become itself. The Epilogue is the manifesto for the dim struggle recorded in the book. If our first reading takes the Preface as its starting point; then our second reading puts its interpretive weight upon the closing section.

In a letter written to Sydney Holland and dated 15 January 1908 Gosse, reflecting on the purpose of *Father and Son*, wrote:

To tell the truth, what I should like to think my book might be - if the idea is not one of too great temerity - is a call to people to face the fact that the old faith is now impossible to sincere and intelligent minds, and that we must courageously face the difficulty of following entirely different ideals in moving towards the higher life. But what ideals, or (what is more important) what discipline can be substitute for the splendid metallic rigour of an earlier age?
There must be found some guiding power, influencing artists, financiers, the meditative and imaginative, the self-centred, and the speculative alike.

It is typical that in the letter Gosse is unable to elaborate fully upon the nature of this 'guiding power'. Could he have meant the guiding principle of individuation? Did he mean that individuals must now find the meaning of their own lives within their own existence, within the strange dynamics and inner necessity of self-realization? What other 'guiding power' exists in the book? (Again, we notice how the claim in the letter conflicts with the Preface of *Father and Son*.) In the same year Gosse wrote to Robert Ross:

I detest nothing so much as the *cliché* in mankind. And more and more personal liberty becomes a passion, almost a fanaticism with me. Less and less can I endure the idea of punishing a man - who is now cruel - because he is unlike other men. Probably if the hideous new religion of Science does not smother all liberty, we are in the darkness before the dawn of a humane and intelligent recognition of the right to differences.

Our second reading of *Father and Son* suggests that the book is very much about 'the right to differences'; and that it offers a somewhat screened autobiographical account of the individuation process in action.

Fortunately, we do not have to choose between the two readings: the historical and the autobiographical. Both possess a kind of validity; both have their place. However, as readers, we can also move along the line of friction between them and come to understand more about the author and his society than, perhaps, was ever intended.

(1983)

CHAPTER NINE

On the Fine Art of Writing Autobiography

> Remembering appears to be far more decisively an affair of construction rather than of mere reproduction... for as has been shown again and again condensation, elaboration and invention are common features of ordinary remembering.

So writes F C Bartlett in a book suitably entitled *Remembering*.

If this is true of remembering, how much more true it is of making autobiography. I use the word 'making' to stress the point, for as soon as one has decided to write an autobiography the process begins; one selects, one edits, one elaborates, one connects. Out of the bewildering multiplicity of remembered sounds and silences, of events and non-events (and half-events), out of anxieties and aspirations, decisions and (as often) indecisions, confrontations and evasions, a web of relationships and non-relationships, one seeks some kind of pattern expressive of the whole confused and labile reality. And then how much of our life seems permanently lost, not only not recorded, but not remembered. Some of our memories, like Lazarus, can be brought back, can rise dramatically and unexpectedly before us; but many, going back into infancy seem permanently to have gone. They live invisibly on the further side of our conscious life, ours and yet not ours at all. One has simply forgotten what colour and design the carpet was, whether X wore jewellery, what the name of one's early companion was - even, in my case, what my first memory is. Much of my own early life seems lost in a kind of permanent winter drizzle. I am envious of those who can enter their childhood like a lit landscape and who can spend hours happily gazing at the radiant details.

It is, I suppose, distinctly odd that I, who have such a poor memory, am so committed to the genre of autobiography. Perhaps it is some kind of compensation for a sluggish memory and a somewhat retarded sense of my own personal past? The latter is, I suspect, more pertinent than the former for I am deeply concerned with questions not of memory but of *identity* (though it is hard to disentangle the two deeply interwined elements); I am concerned with existential questions about *who we were* and *who we might have been* and *who we have become* together with their negative corollaries: *who we failed to be* and *who we might fail to be in the future*. Curiously, the future tense is very crucial in the making of autobiography. By turning back we seek to move forward. We aim to draw the past into the present, either to integrate it or lighten it or to shed it in some way. Our most secret desire is that our life will begin again, less encumbered, as our constructed autobiography comes to a close.

It is this existential element, then, which haunts me, which draws me in, which compels me to write. When this existential element is missing in autobiography, when I find I am reading endless facts paraded by endless egos (as in many typical memoirs where one is offered a mere inventory of things performed, tasks achieved, people met) then my interest plummets to zero in a matter of seconds. Some memoirs seem so leaden they fall from one's hands of their own accord. True autobiographies do not try to impress, they reveal and expose; and, at times, they wield an axe at the ice which can protect us from the depths of our own feeling. I am moved by those autobiographies where one finds a perfect amalgam of poetic recreation and reflexive curiosity. The poetic recreation ensures that the author's experience - or more precisely, the author's *construction* of it - is cast upon my imagination so that I too see it, feel it, and am 'there'. In this respect autobiography works very much like fiction, except, of course, the genre insists on an existential connection, a veritable fidelity between the formal writing and the actual life of the author. The reflexive curiosity refers to that act of intelligent speculation which turns on that recreated experience - recreated through language, recreated through memory - to consider its meaning and its relationship to the broader narrative of existence.

I recently picked up Virginia Woolf's *A Sketch of the Past* and, unlike the weighty memoirs, couldn't put the slim volume down. Like a devout Muslim holding his *Koran* I carried it in my hands all day, reading and rereading many of the paragraphs. What was it about the volume I found so captivating? I am sure it is because it had those qualities of poetic recreation and reflexive curiosity, both working at that level of expression which marks the mature writer, a mesmerising combination of ease and finesse, of spontaneous movement and fitting form. The impressions are recreated with a poetic exactitude so that one experiences the evoked memories but, at the same time, they are examined, diagnosed

103

with a fine analytic intelligence (perhaps one should say psycho-analytic intelligence?). The early memories are very quickly analysed and related to what she calls 'Being' and 'non-Being' and the sense of an emergent almost musical pattern of significance behind the haze of daily experience. And all this is constructed with an honesty which both challenges and chastens one. The reader is left turning in on himself and saying: Could I be as honest as that? Could I narrate my truth (whatever that might be) with the directness that she brings to her own self? And then, one reflects, this is one of the values of autobiography; it confronts us as readers. It releases in our own selves submerged memories and latent rhythms. It turns us spiralling in. Herbert Read, writing his autobiography *The Contrary Experience,* and stumbling upon his first memory at birth (the muffled sound of horses' hooves) went on to claim:

> If only I can recover the sense and uncertainty of those innocent years, years in which we seemed not so much to live as to be lived by forces outside us, by the wind, and trees and moving clouds and all the mobile engines of our expanding world - then I am convinced I shall possess a key to much that has happened to me in this other world of conscious living.

Autobiography may provide us with the lost key to the door of our own existence and a way forward - if the door opens and if we have the courage to go on.

As to my own experiment in autobiography, it is difficult to describe in retrospect. *Icons of Time* is made up of 56 sonnets. Put as starkly as that you can see why I call it now and subtitled it then, an 'experiment in autobiography'. For a sonnet (14 lines, basically in iambic pentameter, with the expectation of rhyme and made up of 100 - 120 words) would seem an odd if not self-defeating form for autobiographical recreation. Certainly, any sonnet-autobiography clearly puts its first emphasis on economic selection and artistic construction. But, surely, you might well ask, doesn't such a formal commitment put barriers across the living gush and flow of memory on which autobiography depends? It is possible. Yet, at the same time, many of the sonnets started as odd lines, broken cadences, fragments, the stray flotsam of life and only slowly made their way towards becoming poems. In fact, many of my poems begin as incomplete lines, jagged notes, rhythmic phrases, solitary images or juxtapositions which, if I am fortunate, evolve into a greater unity. I always find comfort in the genesis of Virginia Woolf's *The Waves* which began, if one can ever say where creative work begins, in the following entry dated Monday February 21st 1927:

Woman thinks
He does
Organ plays
She writes
They say
Night speaks
They miss

Virginia Woolf went on to comment:

I think it must be something on this line - though I can't now see what. Anyway from facts free; yet concentrated; prose yet poetry; a novel and a play.

What was given, then, was a very simple cluster of images, actions and conceptions (all in the present tense) and the emerging apprehension, not too precise, of the kind of literary form they required for their full and final articulation. That is how much writing begins.

My own book *Icons of Time* didn't start as autobiography. It began as a task imposed upon myself as a writer, as a poet. I simply set myself the task of writing some sonnets. I began writing these sonnets, as far as I can remember, about 1980. They engaged with a variety of themes but some of them were about my relationship with my father; they were about a sense of deep unease and guilt I sensed in the relationship. It was these poems which first gave me the idea of writing an autobiography through the form of the sonnet.

In time, the form became a kind of mould in which the unpredictable flow of experience could be caught, cooled, lifted up and made palpable. On a number of occasions I would wake up in the morning to find words running through my mind; I would scribble them down and find, to my amazement, they were sonnet-like utterances, often in fourteen lines and in a rough iambic pentameter. These early morning gifts were not necessarily good from a literary point of view, but they did show that my mind had accommodated the schema and was spontaneously putting it to constructive use.

It became gradually clear to me that my aim was to write a volume of sonnets which was to take my own life as the primary material for poetic recreation. I believe, now, that the sonnet form helped to provide some kind of discipline to unruly and amorphous emotion, not negating it, but somehow essentialising it, giving it an almost ideal representation. In less than 120 words one had the task of dramatising the quintessential lineaments of a particular encounter, collision, trauma, insight, confusion, loss, gain, whatever, as it whelmed up in the animated memory. Such an exacting linguistic regime severely checked any emotional wallowing or any excessive boiling of bad feelings. It forced one in the first twelve lines to pare to the bone and then, in the couplet, to drive the point home. Each poem had to be an act of massive condensation. I wanted the writing to be raw and direct and urgent, but I wanted the expression to be also cut, concise and clear as a jewel: a meeting of memory and artifice.

The more I consciously worked on the sonnet the more I felt I could use the form to fit my own personal ends. I was anxious to capture it to relay issues not in the tradition, experiences absent from the recieved canon. I hoped to express, among other things, rural working-class experience, to express the voice of my father and the painful dislocated rhythms of our relationship, to clarify the crisis in spoken language which haunts and inhibits our society and often divides us into sullen, resentful parts. For I suspected that what I was touching on in my relationship with my father was not merely personal, but characterised thousands of frustrated and unfulfilled lives where the mouth is gagged, the feeling choked and the potential insight swallowed for ever. Some of the central poems, at the heart of the book in the *Father and Son* sequence, are about the failure of the tongue to utter its needs and of lives shut in the cellars of repressive darkness. When I placed the sonnet *Tongue Tied* at the beginning of the sequence it was a deliberate choice.

The writing was an act of therapy - I am sure of that - but I always hoped it was more than that. Nor was it all painful. One of the real pleasures derived, I found, from naming places and giving dates. I had a compelling need to name in full the seminary I went to, to name the Primary School, to raise from obscurity the name of the cottage (Myrtle Cottage) where my Methodist Grandparents had lived in West Runton, as well as the Oak Woods where my Catholic Grandparents lived near Upper Sheringham. The names mattered. For me they had a mythic quality. They marked locations which held those earliest experiences which lie at the root of memory, experiences

106

which are so intimate they seem closer to us than our flesh, haunting far away resonances which can be suddenly released and amplified by a sudden aroma of peach or fig or the sound of a pail clanking or the wind caught in the eaves of the house. The places gave a specificity to the states of consciousness and a geography (moving from Norfolk to Wales to Sussex) essential to the story. At times, also, these same places acted not only as the literal sites of the drama but became metaphors. The kitchen garden at the Oak Woods became the walled garden of eternity; the dyked, horizontal land of Norfolk a symbol of repression; the Downs at Sussex, when the stubble is set alight, an image of spiritual renewal; and the local Safeways a kind of contemporary hell. At these moments the literal places, named and remembered, carried (I hoped) a broader spiritual resonance.

A further satisfaction came in selecting the final sequence for the individual poems, the putting of this one against that to effect a new relationship or juxtaposition. Then when I divided the chosen fifty five sonnets into separate chapters, I felt I was able to discern a pattern in which the individual moments of memory gained a further significance not present in their original state. This enabled a further distancing; and placing. Finally, at the opening of each section I decided to use quotations from Heraclitus to Seamus Heaney to invoke a tradition of reflexivity and introspection of which my own experiment was a small example. The book opens not with my voice but with that of Heraclitus, the man who first gave to the word *psyche* the meaning of *soul*, and who in one aphorism wrote: *I searched for myself*.

John Updike wrote about his own autobiography:

They record what seems to be important about my own life and try to treat this life, this massive datum which happens to be mine, as a specimen life, representative in its odd uniqueness of all the oddly unique lives in the world.

I would like to think something similar applies in the case of *Icons of Time*.

(1993)

107

CHAPTER TEN

The Uses of Autobiography

This chapter takes the form of an interview. In early 1993 at the University of Sussex Dr Robert Graham of the Faculty of Education, the University of Manitoba, Canada interviewed the author about autobiography and its cultural and educational uses. This is an edited transcript of the discussion.

RG: You've been actively involved over the last twenty years in developing the uses of autobiography in education. Could you reflect for a moment on some of the more unusual twists and turns this approach has taken for you since you first began?

PA: I began work twenty-five years ago in a College of Education with a small group of students. Their pieces of written work were eventually included in *Autobiography in Education*. I suppose when I stumbled into the area of autobiography I really didn't know what I was after. I had a basic hunch that unless peoples' lives were connected profoundly with their acts of knowledge, very little could happen that was worthwhile. And I suppose, philosophically, I saw autobiography - even then - as a means of connecting life with knowledge and understanding. So, basically, the students were invited to write, on their own terms, selective accounts of their lives, accounts that they would be willing to share with the group. Yet, even then, I thought I ought to relate what they were writing to the whole field of autobiography. And so while they were writing their own narratives I felt it was my function as a tutor to introduce them to the works of other writers - for example, to Wordsworth's *The Prelude* or Jung's *Memories, Dreams, Reflections*. I hoped that the students would make an immediate connection between their own attempts to recreate a life and the attempts made by other writers in the culture. And that's always remained an absolute driving principle of this work. I think that over the years it has slowly refined itself into a more organized and careful practice. I think I stumble less.

RG: Could you say what those refinements are now since those first beginnings? What do they consist of?

PA: Well, one of them derives from running the MA *Language, Arts and Education* for Arts' Teachers at the University of Sussex. I have cottoned on to the fact that autobiography doesn't have to be verbal narrative. The students on this course use any number of possible symbolic methods to make a representation of their lives: dance, painting, ceramics, video, drama, music. I've also come to realize that autobiography itself breaks down into a whole number of genres. Thus one has, for example, memoirs, apologia, letters, diaries, short stories (that are based on real experiences but actually get transformed in the telling), as well as the more conventional methods of autobiographical narration starting from one's earliest memory and plotting forward. And so on.

RG: There seems to be a premise here that autobiography and art-making are very closely tied together.

PA: No, I wouldn't say that all art-making is autobiography. But take a painter like Rembrandt who painted himself through the whole span of his life from youth to old age. Now when we put these paintings together we have an extraordinary chronological compilation that constitutes a deep visual autobiography. In the same way Munch's collection of paintings *The Frieze of Life* derived from memories of the death of his mother and the death of his sister, and we know they were *intentionally* acts of autobiography and therapy. But I don't think you can go to any painting and say: "Ah, that's autobiography!". That would be deeply reductive. Not all art is autobiography. But art *can* be used to make various kinds of autobiography.

RG: I suppose you would also say that your students (and it seems to me you've been very fortunate in that respect from some of their work I've read) have been amazingly gifted. What do you have to say to the student who comes to you not in that highly-developed state of creativity? How do they also manage to link self to culture and curriculum?

PA: Well, I think now I can actually formalize some of the possibilities.

Anyone entering the arena of autobiography with anxiety could well choose an objective form of autobiography - apologia, say - and then learn from the more adventurous the kind of subjective advances that can be made. On the whole, it's not a problem. Most people *do* want to bring something from their own lives into the arena and to gain some recognition from the experience. This is something the tutor can't do for the individual student and nobody else in the group can. And it actually makes *the student's existence* the condition for starting any intellectual work at all. And that's why I think it is pedagogically so important.

RG: Could you say some more about the models of autobiography that you bring? Are you still using those particular models or others?

PA: You'll be pleased to know - because I remember your criticisms in your book *Reading and Writing the Self* - that I now include feminist work. For example, some of the students have recently made critical studies of Janet Frame's autobiographical trilogy. I've tried to extend the range enormously. The actual structure is rather like this. I give over almost the whole of the first term (we meet one evening a week) to the making of autobiography. Originally, it was a kind of twitching three weeks. Now it's an expansive ten weeks, and I often share some of my own work to show I'm ready to step in the process myself. I give the students a span of time - about five weeks - to make their own experiment in autobiography in whatever medium they wish. In the five weeks that they're making their autobiographies we examine in the weekly formal seminars some established autobiographies and discuss such issues as memory, the art of recreation, symbolism and the different forms of autobiography and their historic development. And then, when the five weeks are up, we have a series of presentations in which, on their own terms, the students actually present to the group what they have made. Then in the last session of the term we consider what's come out of the work, what the problems have been, how it may relate to what artists have made in the tradition, and so on and so forth. We begin to turn conceptually on what we've done experientially. In this way the ground has been prepared for the intellectual work we want to get at in the second term in aesthetics, in criticism and critical theory, as well as in art-making - for on this MA students submit not only critical work but also expressive work in any artistic medium of their choice.

RG: In this particular process where is the link between the memory work, the autobiography work, and the schools or curriculum? Is there any link made or established? Or is this an intellectual quest or endeavour on its own?

PA: Oh yes, it is an intellectual quest in its own right. *It matters*. It matters, first and foremost, because it is an educational process and, in a sense, needs no justification. It is an end in itself. But it also does provide *a metaphor*, at least I hope so, *of good learning*. It sets up an image of education as dialogue, as conversation, as collaborative enquiry moving out from the existential act, which, with various qualifications relating to level and age, can be transferred to any teaching context. But I don't feel I have to over-justify it. The students know it matters by the end of the ten weeks. It really is astonishing. The process has educated me enormously. At first I stumbled, but I now know the process works, if you can get the conditions right. It's extraordinary, it can be truly transformational.

RG: What do you mean by transformational?

PA: Well, some of the students come into the university often over-awed by the fact that they are in a university, terribly lacking in confidence, terribly uneasy about the demands of academic study. I think what this autobiographical work does immediately is to say: *it's not like that at all*. You have to begin exactly where you are. Suddenly, they become scholars of their own narratives, if you like, and that gives them immense heart. Often, they feel much easier after they've brought something personal and difficult into the seminar room and have been able to share it. They become authorities of their own learning, active agents of learning, and then they can extend that to any subject they want, in the same engaged spirit. So a student when about to start a dissertation or an essay may ask: "Well, I can't use the first person singular can I?" and I say, "Well, why on earth not? But, of course, you have to use it well". Suddenly a whole new idea of creative learning comes into play and that can be transformational. Indeed, the autobiographical form can be a very effective way of opening a dissertation or any form of critical enquiry. The autobiographical spirit can enter all intellectual endeavour.

RG: To what extent are you left alone to pursue this work without the kind of administrative queries and questions that I know many of us in colleges of education in North America are subject to, that is, in terms of demonstrating that this work is going to advance the student's understanding, career, etc.?

PA: I think it oughtn't to be too difficult to document exactly why this work is so educational. The self's relation to knowing is crucial. Many theories in the humanities, many theories in psycho-analysis, derive often from a kind of autobiography and acts of deep inner reflection. Freud was analyzing himself when he wrote *The Interpretation of Dreams*; Jung's whole work, is, in part, a projection of the interior landscape of Carl Jung. Many established theories are deeply related to existential quests and are closely bound up with the inner identity of the author. And this is particularly true in the Arts. Picasso, for example, called the vast sum total of his work his autobiography. The same is true of the Mexican artist Frida Kahlo. At the same time, as I have said, it would be wrong to read all art as autobiography.

RG: But in the pragmatic sense that I'm talking about here, many students come to us very much wanting the skills, the know-how of the classroom teacher, and very often find that kind of introspective work not only foreign and alien but very much redundant to their needs, not what they signed up for. How would you respond to that?

PA: Well, an initial reaction might be to suggest that the people you're describing are dispossessed, and they should be given the possibility of repossessing what they have lost touch with. And they've probably lost touch with two things. They've lost touch with the collective life of culture, the whole fabric of inherited culture, what I call the cultural continuum. Our task as teachers is to put our students in engaged and critical contact with their cultural history. The other thing that is fairly obvious is that they have lost touch with their own interior landscape. What

112

we've got to do, therefore, is to put them in an educational context where they can locate their own interior landscape and relate it to the topography offered by the inherited culture. That's our task as educators. That's what it is to teach. Education is never simply a matter of skills. For example, how can one be literate if one reads nothing but tabloid newspapers? One is lost. Such minimal literacy is a new illiteracy. Literacy matters most when it is actually engaging and developing human consciousness. Skills by themselves can never define educational meanings. So, at the very top of the agenda should be a definition of education as genuine inquiry into the nature of things, both human and inanimate, both scientific and humanistic. We need to discriminate sharply between training, which involves the transmission of skills and their application to specific and often utilitarian problems, and education which is the progressive opening out of the mind, a series of thought adventures into the unknown, in which the outcome invariably *trancends the starting point*. The teaching of skills tends to be highly focused on definable ends; education, in contrast, tends to open out into wider and wider vistas of meaning that can't be anticipated in advance of the journey.

RG: But I hope you realize the reason for the question? As I read it, there are certain cultural differences in the way that education faculties in North America differ from those in the UK, wouldn't you say?

PA: I'm not speaking for any orthodoxy, nor am I speaking against skills. I hope that's obvious. In education skills are secondary; they should merely serve the elaboration of the primary quest. That is my deepest humanist view. I couldn't shift from it without betraying what I do.

RG: This leads me back into our earlier topic really, in that I know that the writing of autobiography has been for some students a most alienating experience.

PA: But that's not my experience, as you know.

RG: Certainly. But let me ask you, then, if the experience of writing autobiography is in your view a necessary condition for breaking out of our relationship to history, to the past, and for seeing some sort of way forward. I wonder if you would subscribe to any of that?

PA: Yes, I would. But, of course, I have no experience of doing this work in America or Canada, but only England. You may be pointing to cultural differences of quite a fine kind. But my belief is that there is an innate desire to articulate who we are. It is a kind of natural instinct. Under the right conditions of trust we long to reveal who we are. Indeed, our best relationships are predicated on that kind of trust and almost unconditional acceptance of the other. The purpose of this work is precisely to put students in touch with themselves in relationship to a living culture. That is why in the classroom or in the seminar room one places alongside the students' narratives as many other narratives as one can. So what you set up is not 'a voyage of self-discovery' but more a sense of *my* life, *my* story going into a tapestry of *other lives* and stories which usually *belong together* simply because we're human and because we wish to find out. It may be that you're living in a culture that is egocentric but also one that's paradoxically frightened of self. That may be the source of the blockage.

RG: I think that's a true thing you've said, "frightened of the self". And also that the journey of the self will begin to disturb the world views that uphold that particular version of self. For example, I'm thinking of religion as one of the common blocks to this kind of discovery. dogma orthodoxy doctrine

PA: I don't feel that any of the world religions are necessarily antithetical to what we're doing.

RG: But I was thinking more of the situation that students are placed in when they begin this kind of work; that is, they are faced with confronting their own history and their own religion, and their parents, etc; and many of them are simply quite unwilling to allow that kind of disturbance into their lives.

PA: My instinctive response to that is that, as teachers, we have just got to go on challenging them. That's what Socrates was doing in the market square. He was actually subverting young peoples' notions and inviting them, for the first time, to question, to interrogate both themselves and their society. And that is what education is. If these students want to bypass education then they must be made aware that they're ducking crucial activities.

RG: I'd like you now, if you will, to say a few words about the extent to which some of your students, past and present, have written about or focused in on the way _education,_ as a disciplinary practice in the Foucauldian sense, has affected their bodies. That is, I'm interested in the idea of a corporeal self, in the idea that schooling has done something to them, has perhaps left deep rifts and scars on the way they perceive their bodies, the way they inhabit their bodies, and the way they perceive other bodies as the first way of looking at a self.

PA: Well, that's interesting, because I haven't actually thought about that before and it takes me by surprise. I'm not quite sure how to respond to it. On this Arts course some of the students are dancers and choreographers so for them the idea of expressing their autobiography through their body is completely natural. I find the question hard because anything that affects the mind affects the body. But I'll tell you something that does relate to this. Some years ago a woman had just started to read from the autobiography she had written and tears poured out of her eyes. She looked at me and said, "I can't stay in this room and I can't read this". I was utterly immobilized. I didn't know what to do. I could sense the seconds ticking by and the students looking at me and looking at the desk and the ceiling. Then she stood up. Well, I thought, if she goes out of this room, I've lost her. Then the man sitting on her left said, "You don't have to leave us. Would you like me to read it?" And she said, "Oh, would you?". And so he just took it and read it. And I realised then that if I didn't know what to do - I always claim at the beginning of this work that I'm _not_ a psychotherapist and that it _doesn't_ have to be psychotherapy - that inside any group there's generally someone who knows how to react. And I've learnt to trust not myself but _it_, the process, the collective experience itself, because there's always someone who knows exactly what to do. But the fact that people do occasionally cry does show quite clearly this connecting of the body and the mind and the feelings and it's probably good that at a university a person can cry without making a Californian cult of all holding hands and having to do it. But when it happens because it has to happen, when it's coming from the depths of a person, then I'm pretty sure now that someone will know what to do. That's very important, that the whole transaction is not *in* anyone, it's *between* everybody. The work is vulnerable so it also requires a fairly formal structure and moments of ritual. It is, at all points, collaborative in nature. The work being done isn't located in a single self; it lies between individuals held together by a common and open-ended educational task. It's that transpersonal process that one has to trust.

RG: This sounds very much like a statement of faith here, as a believer in this particular process.

PA: I do believe in it, yes. I've been doing it for ten intensive years on this MA course and it does seem to work. One makes mistakes, but on the whole it is a most distinctive initiation into active learning that then runs through into all the other intellectual and artistic work which follows. But this is a very bad response to your question about the body.

RG: No, I think it is good, because it brought up something very important for me in that you mentioned the word ritual. In my own thinking about this I'm beginning to see that if story and novel become our paradigms for autobiography conceived as a predominantly narrative undertaking, this may be an inadequate analogy in many ways for what seems to happen. A more adequate analogy may be with drama and with ritual which implies certain points of all being together and witnessing and sharing.

PA: Witnessing, yes, I like that word. That's why all the students have to be present. They have a half an hour each to make their autobiographical presentation and they use it however they want. And there is a ritual because we nearly always have wine and eat together. It is something like a symposium in the original Greek sense. There are wonderful origins to what we're doing in both Hellenic and Hebraic culture. It begins with the Delphic oracle's injunction: "Know thyself".

116

RG: And it seems to me a way of creating a sense of community, a sense of solidarity, and that's what takes me back to the idea of drama. For very often we see in drama people at their most vulnerable, displaying themselves and bearing their souls. But we also watch them go through a process of change, we watch them actually change through the process of the drama and I suspect that this is very important for me as an analogue in a way that I don't quite see if I use prose narrative as my analogy.

PA: Yes, that's interesting, isn't it? Because one thinks of drama as a highly vulnerable activity in a public context.

RG: Yes, it seems to me that there is very often, and these are the only words I can use here, a sense of high drama that takes place when people are gathered together to share their stories, and indeed only in the process of making their vulnerabilities public is growth possible. That's a very difficult position of trust to be placed in, and if it's going to work at all I think it's based on a sense of spectatorship as well as a sense of participation, because I get back to that idea of the witnessing of others.

PA: Yes, it's not altogether different from a Quaker meeting, but the context has changed.

RG: In a Nonconformist sense the idea of bearing witness where one stands up in front of the congregation and confesses one's sins, not primarily as a way of gaining absolution but as a way of then being admitted back into the community itself, and so this communal ritual to me is very interesting.

PA: It's an existential transformation, in an educational context, of that kind of experience, isn't it? A transformation which allows for a much wider plurality of possible views, concepts, ideologies, positions and a much richer open-ended dialectic. But as a spirited exchange it's very similar indeed. That doesn't worry me. That simply makes clear the kind of activity it is, and the kind of culture we have come from.

RG: What you're saying with respect to the idea of education, ritual and narrative reminds me of a page in your book _A is for Aesthetic,_ in which you say, "Mythic images are pedagogic images of the highest order. We can adapt the myths to our own changed needs; we can change the narratives, give them a further twist. And where there are gaps we can create new myths". Could you elaborate on that for me, especially on the notion that mythic images are pedagogic images of the highest order.

PA: Well, let's take an example. We find in Plato's *Republic* the image that we're born in a cave, that we are chained to face a wall on which events taking place behind us are being reflected. We innocently read the shadows as reality. That is the human condition, Plato implies. What we have to do and it will be extremely difficult because we're heavily chained is to turn our heads a full hundred and eighty degrees. We have to turn in the opposite direction from which we're naturally looking to discover the truth of our situation. And, of course, Plato then goes on to say that if we do that we experience an enormous sense of alienation from the others chained to face the wall. We're confused and we're disconcerted. And then, he says, one's journey must be to make one's way out of the cave to enter this vast space where the sun is pouring down. Initially, because we have come from such darkness, we can't even begin to comprehend the sun. We can only look at reflections of the light in water. At first, we can just about cope with that. But the journey isn't complete, because until we can actually look up and grasp the wholly impersonal, archetypal truth of the sun, we haven't actually begun to comprehend who we are and how we belong. Now that's a kind of myth. It's a sustained metaphor. It narrates a journey which moves from ignorance to - and the word is pertinent - enlightenment. According to Plato we can become enlightened, but we have to turn absolutely against what we've been given and make our own journey towards the truth. That is an image rich with pedagogic significance. It implies that education is a moving from the known into the greater unknown, painful, yet ending in some kind of enlightenment. This is one of the great imaginal journeys that lie at the root of our culture. Of course, one doesn't have to agree with its underlying metaphysics to grasp its power as a general image of education. Now, there's another point I want to make. One can actually extend, change, and even invert narratives. We can adapt them to meet our changing needs.

118

Take the Biblical story of Abraham and Isaac. Abraham, as you know, is given this great test of faith where he has to sacrifice his son Isaac. Now I've written recently a dramatic monologue where Isaac tells the story. I've taken Isaac out of the known narrative and given him his own space. He tells of this appalling memory. He remembers being taken somewhere by his father, and not knowing why. He remembers the burning fire, and the raised knife and, suddenly, one sees that the story which reveals the nobility of Abraham doesn't look like that at all *when it is told by the son*. I am suggesting one has the freedom to recast the narrative, to offer disturbing angles of perception more in tune with our own insights and judgements.

RG: Peculiarly Post-Modern, by the way.

PA: Very Post-Modern; and one has all the accumulated energy of the narrative to work on, as well as a common understanding of the story and its position in the Bible.

RG: In the concluding chapter of *A is for Aesthetic*, you write, "All that the spirit of Modernism had negated was being rediscovered. The importance of the past tense was reaffirmed, as were the value of place, locality, community, ritual, myth, natural materials, ornamentation, beauty, and the numinous. The extremities of Modernism had brought to birth a conservationist aesthetics". Now you deal Modernism some pretty hard knocks in there, but you never specifically mention the Post-Modern as such, at least in this work, and when you speak of place, locality etc; it seems to me that many of these local narratives now are very much in this spirit of Post-Modernism. How far would you share that perspective, and why have you consciously avoided the use of the term Post-Modern, at least in this work?

PA: It was probably quite a conscious decision to avoid the word Post-Modernism. But, in some ways Post-Modernism is exciting. Its great redeeming feature is that it allows us to engage playfully and idiosyncratically with all the artefacts produced in the past. And that, after nearly a century of Modernism, is very liberating and exciting. But, generally, I don't think there is a sufficient gravity to Post-Modernism. It tends to regard the whole world as a playground to be ironical in. Ultimately, this irony is a form

119

of defence against experience; it's a way of holding back, of being superior, of bypassing what is most difficult and most grave. And what I would like to see is what I call a conservationist aesthetic, that is a more serious return to the past, as possessing forms of wisdom from which we can actively learn. We need symbolism not simulacra. And even where we alter traditional narratives and stories we often need to do so with passion and gravity, not merely with clever grins on our faces. For in retelling we should be trying to get at deeper truths, more adequate representations of what it is to be human. A deeper excavation is necessary. It's Post-Modern with a lower case, if you like, but not Post-Modernist. I feel uneasy about any kind of system that claims total understanding. I am inherently suspicious of all 'isms'.

RG: Then you would agree with Lyotard in his suspicion of all master narratives?

PA: Yes, one should be very wary of total explanations.

RG: I just wanted to know if in some way this levity, this playfulness and this engagement with history that lies behind many Post-Modern literary artists, to what extent this can find a place not only in the education of teachers, but more ambitiously perhaps even in classrooms?

PA: Oh I hope so, yes. One rather hopes this is happening in Britain now under the most difficult of circumstances. There is now a reclaiming of genre, a reclaiming of exemplar, a reclaiming of model, a reclaiming of the past. So by law in the National Curriculum one has to teach Medieval art and Renaissance art. I don't think we've got it anywhere near right with the National Curriculum, but that particular emphasis is good. And it does relate directly to our situation of Post-Modernity.

RG: When we spoke earlier today, in remarking about a paper you have just written about Post-Modernism, you said that you were *in* Post-Modernity but not *of* it. Could you explain how you manage to sustain that perspective?

PA: In *Living Powers* (1987) and *The Symbolic Order* (1989) I argued that Modernism was well and truly over. I wanted to suggest that the Modernist assumption that history had a single unfolding meaning was a disastrous fallacy which encouraged all sorts of avant-garde nonsense. The idea of endless historic progress is now regarded with proper scepticism. So I think for that, and for many other reasons, Modernism crumbled. Therefore, it must follow that we are in a state of Post-Modernity, and that the whole matrix of assumptions that, for the best part of a century, people brought to their cultural experience has suddenly vanished. And, therefore, we're living in a period *after Modernism*. But I don't think that necessarily entails the position of Post-Modernism. It seems to me our period opens up a kind of *elenchus*, a gap, in which we can try and ask all the old questions again. We've got to start again really. But we can't start again from zero, we have to start again in relationship to everything that has existed so far historically.

RG: Do you see some kind of lifeline leading us out of this condition of Post-Modernity? Where might we look for it? Where might we make a start?

PA: Well, I think any real response will take decades to show its true nature. My hope is that we may be able to house ourselves more fully in our imagination so that we can relate creatively to the historical continuum and that we feel a sense of solidarity with that, not alienation. Then we can find our own story within that larger collection of stories. In a similar way, I would hope that we can place ourselves imaginatively inside Nature and see it as part of us and us as part of it, reflecting it back at a higher level. I'm talking about the deep reclamation of historical and ecological dimensions in the arts, in education and in society at large. These are large and difficult matters... but they show where we might make a start.

(1993)

*elenchi pl.
log. prohidükes (socratic elenchus)
                    syllogisliching

Born Rural Working Class

I wrote my first published book in a state of white anger. It was written in two weeks. I scrawled during the day; and in the evening my wife typed it up. It came out in 1969 with the title *English for Diversity*. On the inside cover blurb it said: 'the aim of education is too often seen as that of fitting a child into his society... The author argues that the alternative is to see education as a force for personal fulfilment and social transformation'. I still agree with that (twenty four years later) but am now embarrassed by the book and am hugely relieved that it has been out of print for years.

Yet I stand by the anger which made me write it. I was angry with the conditions in which working class children were expected to learn; I was angry with the assumptions that they were worthy of less; I was angry with the sheer cultural poverty of the schools they had no choice but to attend. And I realise now, as I look through the pages I wrote with such intemperate haste, that I must have been angry with my own background, my own childhood and adolescence.

I came from the rural working-class. In my background none of the arts, as I now understand them, were present. I remember only three books in the house: *Grimm's Fairy Tales, Coral Island* and *Black Beauty* (these, I suspect, must have been presents given to my brother or myself either at Christmas or on one of our birthdays). They were kept upstairs in a large dark cupboard with some unused china and a few tins of fruit, out of daily reach and out of the flow of everyday existence. There were no reproductions in the house with the exception of two small images in our bedroom (a smiling girl with flowers by my bed and two naked boys standing by a fire near my brother's). We heard no live music and virtually no reproduced music either, although I do remember hearing each Sunday *The Billy Cotton Band Show* and (quite often) *Family Favourites* when I visited my grandparents. Needless to say, there was no theatre and not even the notion of expressive dance - that was totally outside the compass of possibility.

122

If, by some impossible accident, a group of dancers had arrived, they would have been regarded as being of the devil's party and quickly shown the door.

Because it was the condition of our existence, we regarded it as entirely normal, as fixed as the sea's movements across the sand or the alternation of the seasons. It was how life was, had always been and would continue to be. Other children who lived in the town occupied the same comfortable and closed world. I do not recall, throughout the length of my childhood, seeing a single child carry a violin or recite a speech from a significant piece of drama. Such events would have seemed socially perverse, an affront to what was expected, an undesirable piece of 'la-de-da' affectation that we were best off without.

In retrospect, what is astonishing is not so much the narrowness of our collective assumptions as the way in which our own formal education did nothing seriously to alter them. It did not attempt to provide what was so obviously missing, those inner symbolic disciplines through which thought and feeling are dramatically enlarged and progressively defined and refined. My education did not seek to widen my cultural landscape; it seemed, contrariwise, to operate comfortably within it.

I went to a Catholic primary school, then for a short time (about two years) to a Catholic Seminary and then from the age of fourteen onwards to a Technical College at Norwich where I did my 'A' Levels and stayed till I was eighteen. During all this time of education - thirteen long years of it - I did not once paint a picture, write a poem, pick up a musical instrument, make ceramics or sculpture, do dramatic improvisation or any mime or dance. During all this time I heard no music, saw no paintings, encountered no significant drama and watched no films, with the exception of a cartoon adaptation of *Animal Farm* which, presumably, was seen by the Catholic hierarchy as being ideologically necessary. In brief, there was no expressive or aesthetic dimension to my learning and, setting to one side the set texts for my literature 'O' and 'A' Level papers, no acquaintance with any of the artistic achievements of Western Culture. At the end of my formal education I was equipped artistically to handle nothing more advanced than the cartoons of the tabloid newspapers or the predictable narratives of soap operas and commercial cinema. At sixteen, my exclusion from real works of art remained so complete it would have been impossible for me to locate or name what was missing. At sixteen, I had simply not heard of Mozart or Beethoven, of Leonardo da Vinci or Picasso; I had not been to a theatre, an opera house or to an art gallery and had little idea of what those places were or why they could possibly matter.

It is true that some of my ignorance depended on my own personal response to Catholicism and the ideological conditions in which it operated, but when one has made the necessary allowances for that, I still feel my own provincial and narrow state of mind was not substantially different from the other students I met later at the Technical College and of most students one would meet now in most sixth form colleges. Fairly recently, I spoke to a small group of students training to be teachers and on mentioning the names of Homer, Virgil and Dante quickly became aware that the majority of them had no idea to whom those names referred. We are, as all the evidence shows, a radically under-educated and emotionally crude, not to say violent, society. We have as a nation a most profound distrust of intellectual curiosity ('curiosity', we say, 'killed the cat') and a fear before the power of Beauty. Not only this, but as a nation we flaunt our aesthetic and educational limitations as if they were assets.

I must now return to the Catholic element in my background. I have said I was given no introduction to the Arts; but it was equally true that I was given no introduction to the Sciences either. What was important was the transmission of Catholic doctrine. At eleven, I could recite whole chunks of the little red catechism (I still can); while at thirteen I could elaborate on many subtle points of Catholic theology. At around sixteen, when I was beginning my 'A' Levels, my religious beliefs began to quiver and gradually break asunder. It was this, and the anxiety which it induced, that took me to the Arts and a kind of speculative thinking which had been either absent or suppressed. The need to understand the nature of my own confused experience drove me to imaginative literature, to poetry and the genre of the exploratory essay. In the gaps between 'A' Level lessons I began to visit small second-hand bookshops in Norwich, blowing the dust off literary volumes and opening the forbidden works in fear and trembling. I read, with an insatiable hunger, whatever directly addressed my swirling inner world. I read thus in an utterly haphazard manner: Dostoevsky, D H Lawrence, Arthur Koestler, Plato, Bertrand Russell, Herbert Read, Stephen Spender, Gerard Manley Hopkins and

Walt Whitman. There was nothing systematic about my reading. It all depended on what my nervous fingers pulled off the dark shelves and the impact of what I first read as I opened the yellowish pages. In this way, I came across Wordsworth's *Tintern Abbey*; I remember reading it with a sense of rapture and identification. I tore the poem out of the book and carried it in my inside pocket for weeks as a magical talisman. It represented much of what I was in search of: an affirmative response to the beauty of the sensuous world of nature, stemming from a genuine experience of illumination. And so the death of my socially determined faith gave birth to a confused but ineradicable search for a more comprehensive and sustaining culture. Much of my criticism of Modernism made earlier in the book has its source here as also the advocacy of an encompassing arts education for all children.

At about the same time, I began to write somewhat furtively, making sure my parents saw nothing of what I scribbled. I needed to make some kind of symbolic order out of the inner dislocation I was experiencing. Every book I eagerly picked up from the second-hand bookshops in Norwich took me further and further away from the assumptions of my home and its routines. I was often smitten with embarrassment and guilt. I still remember the day a branch of the family visited us to find Bertrand Russell's *Why I am not a Christian* on the table in our front-room. I felt such a profound sense of shame and betrayal. Out of the turmoil I found myself writing poetry and while I then thought it was original I can now see, only too clearly, that it derived from the poets I was reading - a curious amalgam of the styles of Hopkins, Lawrence and Whitman. Whatever I read became an immediate and largely unconscious model for my own urgent desire for expression and verbal formulation.

During this time I was studying my 'A' Levels at the Technical College at Norwich. I was studying History and Geography but, for most of the time, such was the nature of my personal crisis, I could only concentrate on the books set for literature (and not all of those). What I needed - I can say it now, I could not have possibly articulated it then - was an institution, not given exclusively to the studying of examination courses, but committed more broadly to the whole, complex, symbolic life of consciousness. I, like nearly all of the students I studied with, needed to be put in touch with all that had been excluded. I needed the chance to hear good music; to see good paintings and sculpture; to witness the dance, theatre and films I had never had the opportunity to encounter. I needed to hear visiting scientists, philosophers, poets, politicians debating current issues and, more importantly, disagreeing with each other. What I required, at that point, was the social experience of authentic culture and true dialectic. This would have done much to make me feel connected to something larger than my uncertain self and would have helped to mitigate some of the guilt and shame I felt for simply wanting to think my own thoughts and wanting to express the stammering life of my undeveloped feelings.

With such a background it is not really surprising that when I began teaching English in Bristol a few years later I wanted to release creative energy in all my pupils and relate them to an infinitely broader symbolic universe. I wanted them to feel what I had so painfully discovered: the power of literature and the pleasures of dialectic. It was the obstacles placed in my path - the banning of drama throughout the entire school, the withholding of 'A' level teaching - that created the anger out of which I wrote *English for Diversity* in two frenetic weeks. As I said at the beginning, it is *not* a good book but I still stand by its central tenet. 'Evidence', I wrote, 'shows that the working-class child is made less intelligent by the circumstances that surround his life. Intelligence, like any other faculty, needs nurturing. It needs to be presented with the means with which to discover and express itself.' Where was the evidence? I didn't document it in the book, but it came partly from my own experience, my own rural working-class background.

(1993)

Myth, Poetry and the Collective Imagination

The social significance of poetry has become obscure. Is it destined to become the first great art form to become extinct? Certainly, it stands in need of some radical revisioning especially as so much published poetry fails so conspicuously to excite the collective imagination. Against prevailing notions of 'relevance' and 'intimate subjectivity' we need to affirm the power of myth and the pertinence of history. Perhaps we need to reclaim the traditional conception of poets as messengers of the imagination who may now have to find ways of working outside the commercial nexus which degrades culture to fast food and reduces the enduring truths of the imagination to mere fads for ephemeral consumption. We need a systematic critique of current poetry and a new orientation; a veritable poetics of the imagination.

CHAPTER TWELVE

The Current State of Poetry

The New Poetry has been recently published by Bloodaxe with an introduction by its three editors, Michael Hulse, David Kennedy and David Morley. Its publication provides an apposite moment to reflect on the current state of poetry. The anthology itself is so densely packed with its fifty five representative poets (the editors confess that their initial list included two hundred and fifty) that it is a somewhat fat and forbidding document. Its sheer volume simply exhausts any impulse to read it whole and entire and so move towards some comprehensive judgement. In this it contrasts dramatically with the volume it deliberately invokes: *The New Poetry* edited by A Alvarez and published in 1962; that volume, so much slimmer and accessible, offered only twenty eight poets and two of those were American. But what *can* be read at a single sitting is the introduction and it is a revealing manifesto, though not exactly in the way intended by the authors, for the expectations it exhibits are as confused as they are fundamentally constricting to the full and proper life of poetry. This is, certainly, not the introduction that one would recommend to an aspiring poet except, perhaps, in a dialectical spirit, as a warning in how *not* to construe the poetic task and, also, how *not* to write.

The main defect of the whole introduction is dramatically visible in its first paragraph, even in its first sentence. It begins: 'Every age gets the literature it deserves'. And then continues: 'As the 20th century opened, the graceful throes of pre-First World War Europe produced a Rilke, the Chicago stockyards an Upton Sinclair, and post-Victorian England the complacency of the Georgian poets but also the turbulent energy of D H Lawrence'. In other words, it begins with a series of breath-taking reductions. It is absurd to state that the 'graceful throes' (whatever they were) of pre-First World War Europe *produced* Rilke; so many forces went to create Rilke, including the force of Rilke himself. *The age* didn't *produce* the *Duino Elegies*; only an individual, working at full emotional and intellectual pressure on all he has ever

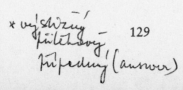

129

known, experienced, imagined, working with (and, at times, against) the whole European culture going back to the Greeks, could create such a master work. To describe the process otherwise is to deny the active powers of the gifted poet, as it is also to diminish what the work has to offer the reader. And the better the work the more it will transcend its age; the Georgian poets may, thus, reproduce the spirit of post-Victorian England but D H Lawrence's work, at its best, created new spaces for the imagination to occupy. And in the case of Lawrence this was often a life-and-death struggle *against* the age. For why, if the age is without spirit and coherence, should the poet merely seek to reproduce it? Why shouldn't the writer connect with remote and distant energies or, like Nietzsche, dedicate the work to the future or, even, to eternity? The dogmatic notion that the age produces the artist denies the innovative creativity of the significant artist as it also diminishes the transformative power of the art created. Indeed, why should any poet struggle with words (write, revise, delete, start again) if the outcome is only to reproduce what already exists?

However, unembarrassed by their facile determinism, our three materialist musketeers continue their theme: 'Throughout the century, the hierarchies of values that once made stable poetics possible have been disappearing. In the absence of shared moral and religious ideals... plurality has replaced monocentric totemism.' And, once again, one puts the book down shocked by the shallow determinism of the analysis and by the clinical jargon. A stable poetics, one wants to say, may have as much to do with the rhythmic flow of breath and the drumming of the heart as with any perceived 'hierarchies of values'. But then, one wonders, what is so terrible *per se* with hierarchies of value? All societies depend upon them, as do all aesthetic judgements. As for 'monocentric totemism', who dare put themselves forward as candidates for this disease? Stand up all those guilty of monocentric totemistic thoughts! Yet *what* does this indissoluble verbal lump actually refer to: a passion for circumference, a desire for unity, an aspiration towards coherence? And *who* does it refer to: Shakespeare, Marvell, Blake, Emily Dickinson, Emily Bronte, D H Lawrence? At one point the introduction would seem to propose that *all* authors before 1958 - yes, *1958* - were deeply stricken by this disease. And this, presumably, further explains why the sparse references to the cultural past are negative and why the great tradition can only appear in inverted commas, as if indicating to the alert reader that 'great'

130

carries with it undesirable hierarchies of judgement while the word 'tradition' inevitably refers to all those earlier misguided works which manifest monocentric totemism. The strong implication is that poets can learn virtually nothing from their predecessors and can pick up only undesirable misconceptions by envisaging their work as belonging to any tradition which transcends the present age. This is a sociological provincialism of a very deadly kind; a poetics of confinement, a politics of suppression.

Having asserted their political historicist position, the criterion for the judgement of contemporary poetry becomes as simple as it is crass and one dimensional: *it must express its age*. From an analysis of the political context of post-Imperial Britain we can discover the most significant contemporary poetry. This is how it is formulated by our three materialist musketeers: 'Life in post-imperial Britain and the death of the national consensus produced (sic) scathing and journalistic work from perhaps the most controversial ironist of the 1980s, Peter Reading'. Indeed, it is clear from the high position conferred upon him in the introduction, as well as the number of poems used to represent his work, that Peter Reading is seen here as one of the pivotal poets of the last twenty years (although any such idea of 'pivotal' is all but alien to the espousal of cultural plurality). Yet the rhetorical claims made for the excerpts quoted seem grossly inflated. And, then, one begins to see that he is viewed as a good poet simply *because* he mirrors his age and is, simultaneously, politically correct in the acceptable ironic Post-Modernist way. Here, without any editing, is the main commentary on Peter Reading from the introduction:

> His (Peter Reading's) post-War English childhood is presented as a series of scenes from Betjemanesque metropolitan life:

> *Pyrex, a pie-dish, deep-lined with apple lumps,*
> *deft in the left hand; with the right, flopping on*
> *   pall of white-dusted droopy pastry,*
> *   slicing off overlaps, jabbing steam-vents...*

> *'52: Mummy paused, wiped a floured hand and tuned in the wireless -*
> *sad Elgar, crackling, then death of our King, George the Sixth.*

Gutter comedy, and tongue-in-cheek linguistic registers (the *Boys' Own*/Biggles Exclamatory), are used to smuggle scathing comments on delusions of British political grandeur:

'56: *going home from the Juniors,*
I read the headlines Suez and Crisis Point -
  crikey! I thought, there must be something
  terribly wrong with the nation's toilets;

soon if the Government didn't act there'd be all kinds of nasties
gushing up out of the drains, Britain would be [is] engulfed.

By the 1980s, Britannia had long ceased to rule the waves; those in power, however, found it difficult to accept the fact.

Far from being 'scathing' the lines are trite and in the case of the Suez pun embarrassingly puerile. *Poetically* there is almost nothing to be said in defence of them (the line breaks seem arbitrary, the rhythms dull, the language banal); but *politically* they do what is required - they record the age, dutifully supplying the necessary dates, names of events (Suez Crisis) and personages (death of George the Sixth). The poem is a political-historical mirror, therefore, it is good. On such a criterion it is amazing that this eclectic bulging anthology does not simply reproduce a page of *The Sun* or *The Daily Mirror*, or, as it is pitted against southern centralism, at least a passage from *The Newcastle Echo* or *The Wigan Voice*.

Yet, perhaps, the most disconcerting element of the introduction is not this rather predictable cultural materialism (now the ruling orthodoxy in English and American Universities) but, rather, the curious shift in the last few pages towards a fashionable Post-Modernism. At first, the engagement with Post-Modernism seems to be largely descriptive, but by the time we have reached the last paragraph it has become a form of advocacy. All very well, one might say; but the problem is that it upends the historicist dogmatism of the opening paragraphs and cleaves the argument (such as it is) into two antagonistic mutually incompatible parts, neither of which are any use to the serious poet. What we have here is not a coherent manifesto or even an explanatory framework but confusion. The muddle demands some further clarification.

The description of Modernism and Post-Modernism is the most facile piece of writing in the whole facile introduction. Indubitably, it is worthy of a place in Pseud's Corner. This is how the two movements ^a become defined:

> Post-Modernism notoriously elusive, can in part be seen as a relish for cumbersome cultural props for their totemic presence alone, without much attempt to see causal connections between larger cultural ideas and the facts of everyday life. Modernism posed Cognitive Questions (asked by most artists of the 20th century, Platonic or Aristotelian, till around 1958): 'How can I interpret this world of which I am part? And what am I in it?' Post-Modernism poses Postcognitive Questions (asked by most artists since then): 'Which world is this? What is to be done in it? Which of my selves is to do it?'

I will leave my reader to struggle with the meaning of this formulation for I am left bewildered by it. I would merely like to raise a few Socratic questions. Out of a list of famous Modernists, say, Virginia Woolf, James Joyce, Picasso, Magritte, Stravinsky, Schoenberg, Beckett and Kafka, who were the Platonists and who were the Aristotelians? How exactly was it that the epistemology changed dramatically around 1958? And, finally, why is the question 'which world is this?' a Postcognitive question and not simply a further cognitive question?

According to our three materialist musketeers the poet Paul Muldoon is the presiding figure of this new Post-Modernist relativity. Attempting to clarify this, they write that the relativism, which they say is still gaining ground, currently relates to: 'a realisation that ideas of meaning, truth and understanding are in themselves fictions determined by rhetorical forms and linguistic terms used to express them.' At this point in their argument it is unclear whether our editors are describing *or* advocating - for, surely, such a position cannot be compatible with the dogmatic one of history creating meaning, of the age determining the art? If history is merely a figure of speech where can the historically determined needs and values lie? One can be a cultural materialist *or* a deconstructing Post- Modernist; but, surely, not both at the same time? Yet it would seem that our materialist musketeers secretly long to shed their historical skins and re-emerge as subversive Post-Modernists. Perhaps, they too must keep up with the demands of the age, even if they are reconceived as rhetorical constructions.

Their re-appearance at the end of the introduction as relativists and pluralists of the Post-Modern persuasion is whole-hearted:

> The work collected here documents poetry in the British Isles at last responding to the imperatives of the times. It is writing that is alert to the fact that British poetry's prevailing modes - in our period, social and realist - are species of fiction like any other and that, consequently, the 'truth' or 'understanding' promised of poetry are largely fictional too.

What is utterly unclear is how they have made the step that takes them from the first paragraph to the last - for under Post-Modernism the march of historic causality collapses into the dance of the signifier; in a quite radical sense there can be no sustaining, unfolding, evolving, justifying, historical process. As the above quotation shows, truth and understanding (like the great tradition before them) go into quotation marks as utterly problematic while the tropes and the metaphors come into their own. What is, finally, so intriguing and so damaging is that on closer inspection one sees the old materialist language at work in the passage above ('the imperatives of the time', 'in our period, social and realist') in an intellectual formulation which, if it were to be taken seriously, utterly negates it. Unwittingly, it demonstrates a blind confusion which, ironically, expresses the imperatives of our age only too well, but, as a vehicle for guiding understanding or releasing the full authentic life of poetry it is powerless, worse, it is spiritually and culturally repressive. It shuts the doors on consciousness and its subtle elaboration through poetic activity. When even the word 'understanding' has to be placed in those Post-Modern quotation marks the arts, inevitably, become a kind of game, a pack of cards, a hall of mirrors, a book of spoofs. This, of course, is not exactly where the three musketeers would have us go but at the end of their turgid introduction this is where the arrow is pointing. Here it is called eclecticism and pluralism, but take the political prejudices out and we have arrived; an even better name for the place, to link it to a cultural past, is the Waste Land. Perhaps, poets would be better off responding against the imperatives of the time? Would it not be wiser to seek an infinitely broader framework for their socially fragile activity, not just 'social and realist'? And wiser also to restore rather than dismantle the old connection between art and understanding, between poem and meaning, between

rababrely, bombastically 134
(ungracefully)

common word and common world? Perhaps, what is needed is an entirely different agenda? At least, the argument should be made, especially as the position of poetry, in our technological civilisation, remains, for the most part, shockingly bleak.

Unquestionably, the making and publishing and performing of poetry is in a precarious state. It may not become extinct in the 21st century but it may well survive in Britain only as the personal commitment of a few hundred people; it may continue as a specialist predilection, a kind of small frenetic club on a par with associations devoted to steam-engines or antique furniture. It would have no visible presence in the diverse collective transactions of the culture; the vast majority of the populace would have no interest in what was being written and, indeed, have virtually no knowledge of it. As I write these lines I realise, with a sudden jolt, that I am not outlining the imminent future of poetry but describing what actually exists now. Poetry is already a small club, a sub-culture - essentially cut off from the collective life of the society. A typical book of poems by a serious poet is now, more often than not, funded by a bureaucratic grant (as is the Bloodaxe volume of *The New Poetry)* and can expect to sell only a few hundred copies; a typical poetry journal *(Poetry Wales, New Spokes, Outposts)* will sell between 200 and 600 copies and most of its readers will be made up of poets, either publishing or hoping to publish in the same journal. The situation would seem to be little better in America, where according to the American Poet Laureate, Joseph Brodsky, 'a standard commercial publishing house, printing this or that author's first and second volumes, aims at 0.0001 percent of the entire population'. In Britain we could possibly add some further noughts to that diminishing figure. Whatever the exact details - and whatever the obvious exceptions to the dominant trend - we would seem to be into remote decimal points and ever decreasing fractions.

But, it might be objected, what about the immense success of current Poetry Competitions? Every week another competition proudly announces itself and confidently awaits a veritable avalanche of entries. Doesn't that indicate health and vitality? On the contrary, I believe the rash of Poetry Competitions across the land indicates exactly the chronic marginalisation of the art form. The much hyped competition is, in fact, the poetry ghetto in its most elaborate and flamboyant disguise. The whole activity, including the actual flow of

135

money from the losing poets to the winning poets, spirals within itself; poets judge poets, and the winning poets read (where performance exists) to fellow poets (and a few friends). An intensely active small group feeds off its own resources, material and symbolic, and has the comforting illusion that all is culturally well. But what stands out to any disinterested observer is that the great British public is all but entirely absent from the feast. In brief, the Poetry Competition is a symptom and not an answer. It is a surrogate activity. It offers a simulacrum of cultural engagement in exchange for the real thing.

Although it is far from easy to grasp, it would seem that the status of poetry as sub-culture (as cosy club or febrile ghetto) comes further to shape and narrow the expectations of the group itself. The public indifference 'out there' slowly materialises as the negative shadow within. The unloved thing becomes unlovable. Many poets thus come to envisage their own role as small, partial, marginal; a note of self-denigration, irony, cynicism and wilful obscurantism comes to prevail. The traditional high expectations of the poetic function - as defined, say, by Coleridge, Keats, Blake, Eliot, Yeats and Kathleen Raine - are mockingly discarded and more limited and mundane ones take their place. In some cases the matter of poetic content contracts to a question of style which, in turn, quickly dissolves into the art of the opaque, the self or ghetto-referential or merely the clever-clever. One has only to pick up *The Times Literary Supplement*, almost at random, to find example of what I am talking about. Indeed, from its pages alone one could quickly compile (for other poets, of course) the *Definitive Anthology of Utterly Obscure Poems* (and probably secure an Arts Council grant for its publication). In other cases some content remains but it becomes wedded to the nasty, the brutish and nihilistic (examples can, also, be found in abundance in the *Times Literary Supplement);* and, in one notorious case, poetry simply becomes an up-market form of pornography. Here, of course, the poetry *does* have a highly explicit content (and also quickly finds a commercial publisher) but one so calculated and so restricted that, once again, it confirms the collective judgement that poetry is little more than a trivial pursuit, or even worse.

I am claiming that the scope of much contemporary poetry (not all, by any means) is too narrow and that the range of register - ironic, flat, jokey, journalistic, minimal, 'social and realist' according to our three editors - is, likewise, too restricted. There is a fear of

136

deep exploratory thought and of vulnerable feeling; there is a fear of experimentation, a suspicion with regard to the more ambitious modes of writing. A kind of corrosive scepticism is at work. Poets, as it were, are clinging to prose. Many of the poems written may (alas) mirror our age but in serving such a limited function (a plastic Donald Duck mirrors our age) they further erode any claim that poetry can make on the attention of the wider civilisation. Ironically, the poetry comes to justify the indifference it is given and in this way the discriminating social judgement becomes, uncannily, vindicated. The unloved becomes unlovable.

How can a broader framework for poetry be developed? I would like to offer a few positive suggestions.

Firstly, it would be liberating if the fashionable political taboo on Western European Culture was, once and for all, lifted. It would give the aspiring poet a sense of a long historic culture within which to work and within which to rebel; it did this for the first literary modernists, Ezra Pound, T S Eliot, James Joyce and Virginia Woolf; but the problem with them is that they were unforgivably 'elitist' in their possession of it. Look, for example, at a typical page of Ezra Pound's *Cantos* or the quotations at the front of *The Four Quartets* and you encounter an implicit disdain for the common reader. The obscurities are consciously cherished and any translations from the Greek or Latin or Italian or Chinese conspicuous by their absence. There can be little doubt that the loss of the broad audience for poetry began around this time and - with a few exceptions, like that of John Betjeman and Philip Larkin - has never recovered. But the rank snobbery and general disdain cultivated by the early literary Modernists for the general reader is, needless to say, not a necessary attribute of possessing an historic tradition; and it is precisely this sense of being a member of a greater encompassing culture which the contemporary poet needs to transcend the insularity and low materialism of our time, as well as the deceptive attractions of autistic self-definition.

By historic tradition I do not mean a prescribed set of canonised texts but, rather, a shifting pattern of diverse individual work and diverse genres. A historic tradition provides a range of exemplars and expressive possibilities; it offers a resonant collection of stories and metaphors (which can be cast by the contemporary poet, again and again) as well as a compendium of metrical forms (which can be experimented with, extended, modified and, at times, discarded - except that whatever may take their place will then always be deeply affected by them). Tradition means having a thousand eyes and of being party to innumerable conversations and paradoxes. The disturbing fragmentary energy of *The Waste Land* depends on its relation to a long historic culture which is evoked and quoted in the very language of the poem; the vision of D H Lawrence depends likewise on the inherited verbal power of the King James' Bible and Non-Conformist hymns (which, in turn, derived from the rhythms and images of the Bible); while the recent work of Thom Gunn, engaging courageously with the experience of Aids in California, is unthinkable without Elizabethan metrics on which the work is formally constructed. A tradition - and the European tradition is constantly expanding as it continues to react with all that surrounds it - offers the materials and means of individual liberation, however that liberation may be defined.

Secondly, it might well be better for the current state of poetry, if poets engaged more fully with ideas. There has been a strong fashion for the best part of this century that poetry should eschew abstraction; that it should stay clear of conceptions and embody its meaning in sharp images and salty words. The favoured form, as a consequence, has been the honed lyric, concentrating on an impression, creating a mood, hinting at significance. The question is whether this particular approach (not the only one in play, it is true), for all its initial cleansing effects has not contracted, too severely, the range of possible poetic content. The lyrical mood-poem, dependent on the radical compression of language and the simple path of a few razor-sharp images, precludes other initiatives: the development of a speaking voice with a distinctive idiom, for example, or the elaboration of the connections between the highly concentrated 'moment of being' and the world, physical, metaphysical, historical, to which it belongs. The demands of the convention check introspection and narrative flow; they tend to close down enquiry, amplification, argument. They conspire against narrative poetry, satire, dramatic monologue, dramatic dialogue, not to mention epic and the saga.

Yet a mere glance at the European tradition reveals that a relationship between poetry and philosophy can be profoundly productive for both partners. Dante was steeped in the theology of Aquinas, Blake in the writings of Swedenborg, Coleridge in the work of Kant and Schelling, Hopkins in the formulations of Dun Scotus, Rilke in the philosophy of Nietzsche, Brecht in the political writings of Marx and Kathleen Raine (to take a contemporary) in the long tradition of Platonic and neo-Platonic thinking. The engagement with philosophy can expand the poet's range of understanding as it can also provide, as it did for Dante and Rilke, a frame-work for shaping and evaluating the dramatic action of the emerging poem. Clearly, in such matters there can be no prescription, but there can be, what the poetic milieu tends to rule out, a profound expansion and imaginative animation when poetry opens into philosophical speculation and the field of ideas (which now would include an engagement, say, with the New Physics, with the Evolutionary Debate, with Medical Ethics, with Ecology). Any such expansion would necessarily bring with it a new interest in those poetic forms which evolved to shape and sequence thought, argument, paradox: the forms of metaphysical poetry, of Augustan poetry, of Classical Poetry and the forms of dramatic narration.

Defiantly, challenging the age, the contemporary poet needs to adopt a public role; to see him or herself as one symbolic agent in the innumerable transactions of collective life. The case of Tony Harrison comes to mind. Here is a poet who operates outside the poetry club and the ghetto, disdaining its coded messages. His work ranges from moving autobiographical work to political satire, to the poetic examination of the *fatwa* passed on Salmon Rushdie, to the human horrors of the Gulf War; it has included a profound apprenticeship to the past in the reconstruction of Greek satyr plays and the translation into telling couplets of the classical drama of Racine and, most recently, the attempt to depict the reality of Alzheimer's disease. The work had been transmitted through diverse media; not only through readings and publication, but also through radio, television and the theatre. And it has gained, unquestionably, a large audience of people (not just the small group of fellow poets) who urgently want to understand the issues of their own time and wish to reconnect with the narratives of their own historic past. Here is a contemporary example of a poet making contact with a long tradition, of experimenting with a variety of forms (but especially the couplet), of engaging with disturbing contemporary dilemmas and also, of finding a responsive general audience outside the ghetto.

A public role can exist for the poet. Tony Harrison's work shows the way but it only expresses a small portion of the themes and forms which must now be opened up. There is so much more to be brought in, so much more to be brought back. For that to happen there must be a general broadening of categories, expectations and practices in the poetry world itself. If that happened, then the world might turn round and listen and be transfixed.

There are signs that what I am advocating may be happening, particularly in America under a movement that has been named The New Formalism, Expansive Poetry or the New Narrative Poetry, and is now gathering momentum there. Their position has been elaborated in two uneven volumes, both of which read like manifestos, *Poetry after Modernism* (1991) edited by Robert McDowell and *Expansive Poetry* (1989) subtitled *Essays on the New Narrative and the New Formalism* edited by Frederick Feirstein. The content of these volumes is not consistently high and much of it relates to the specific context of American poetry with its vast creative writing programmes and their institutional connection to the Universities. The allegation is that the Universities are forming in America the protected ghetto for poetry and, thereby, robbing the broader culture as well as promoting narrow intellectual orthodoxies. As this is not the case in England, and as I am not aiming to review the books, I will concentrate here on the positive side of their advocacy as it bears on the argument I have presented so far. I believe we have much to learn from the fresh shock of their polemic.

The New Formalists mount a formidable and unified attack on what they see as the typical, short, free-verse poem of the age. The offending poem is described by Dick Allen in a chapter called *The Emperor's New Clothes* as follows: 'the highly charged, small, concrete, personal, colloquial, descriptive, usually free-verse lyric which does not deal directly with general matters'. The problem, they argue, is *not* that free-verse is unacceptable but that it restricts; that, ironically, it represses other ways of feeling, seeing and imagining. In the attempt to locate the nature of this restriction, Wyatt Prunty analyses quite brilliantly the tendency in imagistic free-verse to isolate experience from its historic manifold. 'When an image is used', he writes, 'relations rather than events are evoked. The projection of a temporal predicament into an atemporal image..........voids the problem of time rather than addressing it'. Against this practice, he asserts the alternative practice of employing myth. He claims:

Freezing a temporal predicament through the use of myth is a different matter because myths are stories and thus have duration: they carry histories. Images are often extensive, parts in networks of meaning, but characteristically their significance is not born of the past or of a supposed past. When an allusion is made to myth, the reader familiar with that myth suddenly recalls a chain of events: time is gathered.

This concern with 'duration', with chains of events recognised in the historic imagination, would seem crucial to the Formalist's general concern with both narrative and the place of story as well as their desire to address a broader public.

Their conception of the social significance of the poet relates, in part, to the notion of historic time and collective memory. Dana Gioia in one of his contributions to the debate writes:

Meter is also essentially a pre-literate technology, a way of making language memorable before the invention of writing. Trained poet-singers took the events and ideas a culture wanted to preserve - be they tribal histories or magic ceremonies - formulated them in meter, and committed these formulas to memory. Before writing, the poet and the poem were inseparable, and both represented the collective memory of their culture.

It is as if the Expansive Poetry movement wanted to reclaim their ancient position in entirely new circumstances. Dick Allen, for example, dismissing most contemporary poets as 'small artists singing only in minor keys', claims that the traditional concept of the poet should be reconsidered:

The concept sometimes allowed the poet, particularly the mature and proven poet, to take on the role of spokesman for his people, his country, his age. If he spoke sound words of wisdom; if he attempted to teach as well as sing; if he could translate major concepts, philosophy, understandings of the hard and soft sciences into living, feeling language the layman could understand and be moved by; if he offered vision and perhaps even some prophecy; and if his art was equal to the task of all this *weight* in poetry, he might well be praised rather than scorned.

The public philosophical nature of art is stressed as also is the engagement with intellectual movements and changing ideas.

The writers are acutely aware of how much of their position contradicts the dominant poetic orthodoxies of the USA and delight in their defence of intellect and high culture. Frederick Turner is at his polemical best in exposing the current anti-intellectualism of 'the intellectuals':

> All contemporary poets are required to be able to demonstrate some credentials of anti-intellectualism: at least a contempt for technology and the exact sciences, and an ignorance of contemporary philosophy, at best, and especially in America, a complete oblivion to cultural and intellectual history, the fine arts, and literature before 1920. Generally speaking contemporary poets are supposed to regard the enterprise of at least *western*, if not *all* high culture, as disastrous failure. It is as if through a sort of cultural and social nonconformity a poet can achieve that genuine artistic nonconformity called originality; but too often the former is a *substitute* for the latter.

Unlike our three musketeers, this is not a man to put the great tradition of Western Culture in equivocal inverted commas. The commitment to *ideas* and the need for *content* in poetry is clear, unapologetic and striking.

At the heart of this American poetic movement is a recognition of the crucial place of artifice in the making of poetry. They are all bored by the poetics of the naked self and the howling infant; they are tired of the standard spilling of words on the page dignified by the concept of 'free-verse'. In a world of extreme expressive poverty and verbal narcissism, they call for the re-animation of myths and stories, for the restoration of a variety of demanding poetic forms, for the creation of masks and personae. According to Frederick Turner: 'all the masks are denied to the modern poet, for instead of having at his disposal the rhythms and tone of other eras, and a repertoire of contemporary poetic stances, he has only one, which is his own'. He elaborates the idea at a later point, 'with meter a poet can explode into all those selves and fictions he yearns for, and which, in our age, he often lacks so badly that he murders himself out of starvation for them'. In the place of the autobiographical free-verse lyric, the new formalists insist on the need for a dramatic expansion; a poetics based on memory, on

142

artifice, on intellectual engagement, on the power of myth and story and on the function of the poet as a symbolic integrator and transmitter of meanings.

The condemnation of the current condition of poetry in America is severe and most eloquently formulated by one of the leading figures in the group. In his essay *The New Formalism* Dana Gioia relentlessly exposes the poetic cultural milieu of America with an unnerving precision.

These poets have grown up in a literary culture so removed from the predominantly oral traditions of metrical verse that they can no longer hear it accurately. Their training in reading and writing has been overwhelmingly visual not aural, and they have never learned to hear the musical design a poem executes. For them poems exist as words on a page rather than sounds in the mouth and ear. While they have often analyzed poems, they have rarely memorized and recited them. Nor have they studied and learned poems by heart in foreign languages where sound patterns are more obvious to non-native speakers. Their often extensive critical training in textual analysis never included scansion, and their knowledge of even the fundamentals of prosody is haphazard (though theory is less important than practice in mastering the craft of versification). Consequently, they have neither much practical nor theoretical training in the way sounds are organized in poetry. Ironically this very lack of training makes them deaf to their own ineptitude. Full of confidence, they rely on instincts they have never developed. Magisterially they take liberties with forms whose rudimentary principles they misconstrue. Every poem reveals some basic confusion about its own medium. Some misconceptions ultimately prove profitable for art. Not this one.

Who, reading this sharp indictment of America, can claim that it is significantly different here in England? And who can claim that the English Universities, the Literature Departments with their commitment to ideological theory, have done anything but add to the symbolic impoverishment and general practical ignorance?

The movement calls itself expansive because it wishes poetry to expand outside the gates of the University and educational establishments. It wants poetry to be on the streets, in the offices and the supermarkets, working as now an integrating, now a subverting energy. The American Formalists look back to a time when poetry was widely read (as it would seem to have been in Britain before the First World War and the outbreak of Modernism) and seek to draw back the missing audience. They aim to do this through the cultivation of story and myth, through the use of established forms, through an engagement with substantial issues.

The argument seems, at once, both impossibly grand and yet entirely necessary. *Here* is a movement in excess of the age, defying its imperatives and its raging orthodoxies (as they exist in America, for there is certainly more recognition of form and narrative in Britain). I believe it clears back some of the boulders in front of the cave and generously beckons poets to the new ground except, of course, this ground is not new (it only feels that way because of our current alienation); it is, in fact, ancient ground which has been tilled and planted down the ages. For narrative is as old as human life, so is something like meter, so is the profound human curiosity about meaning (about space and time and life and death) and the need to share it. What is being called for, then, is a return to sources and a return to symbolic basics. Where else at the end of the 20th century could we have gone? I believe that the poetry ghettos on both sides of the Atlantic have much to learn from these writers. It has been a deep confirmation to discover their proclamations and their proposals for the making of poetry in our time.

(1993)

CHAPTER THIRTEEN

Personae and the Art of Retelling

Humanity will increasingly be turning back to itself, increasingly
contemplating its entire past, searching for a key to its own enigma,
and penetrating, through empathy, the soul of bygone generations
and of whole civilizations.

Czeslaw Milosz

For too long now we have been powerfully subjected to a convention
- and a convention it is - that the poet is primarily concerned with the
articulation of direct feeling and that what is created is then a work
of 'self-expression'. In the last three decades in Britain and America
this prevalent notion has given birth to an over population of what
can be most accurately described as 'mood-poems'. Indeed, there are
good reasons for claiming that the mood-poem is the dominant poetic
form of our times, not only the characteristic product of creative
writing classes but also the favoured style of most poetry journals
and poetry volumes.

How best to typify the mood-poem? It is generally a work of
partially sublimated autobiography; it tends to be rather modest in
scope, generally short and slightly elusive or ironic in meaning. The
aim of the mood-poem would seem to be to express a state of
subjective feeling, often related to a shift in some personal relationship,
which is recreated through a series of visual impressions and then
simply left. The mood-poem represents a kind of verbal impressionism.
In its private nature it bears a certain resemblance to the utterance of
those undergoing psycho-therapy except that in the manner of
communication it is much more controlled, more frugal, more distant,
more placed. It is not generally raw; it is not a primordial scream or
an elemental sigh. The mood expressed, though, is often tinged with
negativity; it is vaguely depressed, ironic, self-deprecating, disillusioned
in a fairly civilized manner. It avoids extremity and favours control.

The language of the mood-poem tends to be that of clipped
conversation. It is often idiomatic, unadorned, imagistic, contemporary and laconic. It avoids excess as it avoids experimentation.

It is deeply suspicious of too much artifice, too much style. One can define the mood-poem best through antithesis. It is the opposite of complex, metaphysical, abstract, epic, innovative. It could be said to operate in a deep cultural exile; it forges few connections with other disciplines of thinking, it bears few allusions to the historic past, it carries few references to the collective experiences of humankind. Any energy the mood-poem possesses is hermetically sealed inside the impression it would create. It is an abbreviation of isolated intimacy and content to be merely itself. It thus avoids the disturbance of intellectual questioning and eschews, for the most part, reference to science, technology, engineering, law, biology, politics, commerce, medicine, theology, philosophy and the dilemmas and possibilities they represent for human existence at the end of the 20th Century.

Historically, the mood-poem can be seen as a poem of deflated Romanticism, of Romanticism at the sparse edge of technological society, shorn of its lofty rhetoric; Romanticism with a simple lower case 'r'. It expresses an isolated subjectivity as the vast mass of confused impersonal civilization moves elsewhere. It is, inescapably, a manifestation of the predicament of poetry in a technological age but the question remains as to whether it is the only or best manifestation possible and, if not, what other expressive moves are available to the poet. Recently, R S Thomas in a chance remark gave an historical frame for our understanding of the plight of poetry. He suggested that John Donne was the last poet in the British tradition to be able to encompass in his poetic work the expanding elements of his own civilization. Donne had, or so the argument goes, a language at his disposal sufficiently broad, subtle, inventive, metaphysical, to explore and integrate, with considerable tension, the diverse cultural pressures and thought-adventures of his time.

T S Eliot in his theory of the dissociation of sensibility made a similar point about the metaphysical poets. The poets of the seventeenth century, he observed, 'possessed a mechanism of sensibility which could devour any kind of experience'. He went on to say: 'our civilization comprehends great variety and complexity, and this variety and complexity, playing upon a refined sensibility, must produce various and complex results. The poet must become more and more comprehensive, more allusive, more indirect, in order to force, to dislocate if necessary, language into his meaning'. Eliot's comments

146

are often a hidden manifesto for his own writing but they also invite us to look at much of our contemporary poetry to discover that it is neither comprehensive in its range nor complex in its approach. The mechanism of sensibility which devours disparate experience into a further synthesis is, for the most part, absent. Is it possible that the diagnosis made by Eliot remains accurate? Is it possible that, since the metaphysical poets, poetry has been journeying down an ultimate cul-de-sac which has ended in the modest, professionally shaped, mood-poem? Could it be that the poet forfeiting, for a variety of reasons, the wider structures of civilization (law, commerce, politics, theology, technology etc.) has become a specialist in private feeling and a historically unlocated subjectivity?

These are disturbing questions calling for further and finer analysis. Here I can only add a small piece of autobiographical evidence, analyse it and move towards advocating an alternative approach which relies more on collective narrative and on public memory and which seeks imaginative transformation by working within the whole continuum of historic culture; an approach which if it is not, because of its moral and metaphysical seriousness, Post-Modernist is distinctly post-modern, as it is also post-romantic. An approach which is, indeed, now becoming widely employed and which may, if we are fortunate, place the mood-poem in one small corner of what should be the large and busy Stock Exchange of poetry.

When I was about seventeen and suddenly (and unaccountably) keen to practice the art of poetry I came across D H Lawrence's *Preface to the American Edition of New Poems*. It was akin to a revelation. Here was a writer proclaiming the utterance of the new and unpredictable against the established poems of the dead past. What mattered, urged Lawrence in his relentless musical drum-beat, was to allow the poem to issue out of the immediate experience so that it was a symbolic gestalt of the body and mind of the actual writer. After its spontaneous expression all that was needed was a little editing, a removal of any banality or cliché which had attended the flow of language. Lawrence wrote:

> All the laws we invent or discover - it amounts to pretty much the same - will fail to apply to free verse. They will only apply to some form of restricted, limited un-free verse...
> The utterance is like a spasm, naked contact with all influences

at once. It does not want to get anywhere. It just takes place...
We do not speak of things crystallised and set apart. We speak
of the instant, the immediate self, the very plasm of the self. We
speak also of free verse.

These were the claims of Lawrence and to a young man, with
virtually no knowledge of the cultural past or any real knowledge of
poetic form, they were deeply persuasive. They flattered my ignorance
for they made it seem that any knowledge of technique or any
knowledge of the past would merely impede or corrupt the natural
flow of language as it articulated the moment of emotion. I was
enthralled. It gave me permission to be a poet. It gave me a kind of
philosophy built on the foundations of 'self', 'spontaneity' and
'sincerity'. In its rejection of the notions of apprenticeship, tradition,
imitation, collective knowledge, artifice, history (Lawrence had written
in 1916 to Catherine Carswell: 'Let the dead bury the dead. Let the
past smoulder out. One shouldn't look back') it conformed with some
of the essential imperatives and sentiments of Modernism and
Progressivism; and as far as I was concerned, that was fine as well.

Lawrence remains, in my view, a significant writer and there are
liberating elements in his manifesto for 'free verse'. Yet, as time passed,
I became more and more critical of the argument being made. I am
convinced now that as it joined other similar arguments and
orientations (many deriving from psycho-analysis) it led to that
isolation and subjectivization of experience which I have already
described. The problem with the theory is that it is excessively simple.
It possesses a kind of puritanical zealousness which smothers critical
reflection. At the heart of Lawrence's manifesto lies the notion that
self and language are transparent forces: the natural self is simply
made visible through the act of spontaneous writing. Self and
expression become one: 'self-expression'. And, furthermore, it is a
self-expression in which much in the collective culture has been
removed for it had been judged in advance as 'petrified' or, as we
would say in today's jargon, 'irrelevant' and 'outmoded'.

Yet a moment's introspection throws profound doubt on such a
description. First of all, with regard to our daily experience of ourselves,
it is often opaque, discontinuous, intermittent, submerged. We are often
more and sometimes less than we can say. Our experience, being labile
and multiform, resists instant formulation. For this reason, as I will try

to show, the use of masks and personae may allow us to capture more than naturalism can and also enables us to place our experience within a collective rather than a private space. Secondly, we also know from bitter experience that language itself invariably resists the enterprise of immediate reflection. In writing, words are not like mirrors in the bathroom but more like combustible fluids in the alchemist's laboratory. They enter the arena as creative agents, not simply reflecting but developing, distorting, changing, shifting, deepening and, in nearly all cases, altering the initial transaction. Words can never become 'the plasm of the self'; nor are they 'naked' (one of Lawrence's favourite adjectives) simply because they come marked by all their previous uses. This observation brings us to the heart of the matter and to the central fallacy of 'self-expression' and to the residual poverty of the contemporary mood-poem. The truth is that we are *cultural* beings who seek transcendence. We live in historic moments of time, where we struggle to make clear our difficult sense of vision, our exacting sense of values; and to do this we have no choice but to employ the inherited gift of language with as much skill and daring as we can lay hold to. Perhaps a way of stating the same conclusion is to say that our most *natural* possession is, paradoxically, our *cultural* inheritance. As the Polish poet Czeslaw Milosz puts it: 'If reality exists, then how are we to dream of reaching it without intermediaries of one or another sort, whether they are other literary works or visions provided by the whole past of art?'

It has taken me some years to move away from D H Lawrence's defence of free-verse and the influences it exerted on me. It is true that the poet must be alert to the life of feeling; but even here, as we have seen with the typical subject-matter of the mood-poem, the problem is that the feelings are conceived in relationship to a solipsistic self and not in relationship to a highly differentiated civilization, neither in relationship to technology, politics, medical advance, commerce, science, nor in relationship to the collective metaphors, myths, fables, concepts and narratives which make up the daily symbolic transactions of society. The feeling is placed *in* the person as an isolated private container rather than in a network of relationships *between* the elusive self and the mobile culture.

In opposition to Lawrence I would now want to say that poetry is best seen as being made (inside specific traditions) and as being addressed to the imagination of the culture (embodied in whoever might respond to it) where it seeks some realization of truth. This involves a radical

149

shift from 'self', 'spontaneity' and 'sincerity' and a move towards 'skill', 'tradition', and the 'representation of truth'. Whether a poem is sincere or not, spontaneous or not, expresses the self or not, is beside the point - except in autobiography. A poem could be all of these things and at the same time execrable (as all editors and judges of poetry competitions hardly ever admit but collectively know). <u>What matters is whether some truth in the complex manifold of life is being expressed</u> and whether <u>that truth is artistically compelling to the human imagination</u>. With these public categories before us I would like to elaborate more fully on the use of personae and the art of re-telling.

How, then, to turn from the private subjectivities of the mood-poem to an art that has a more public disposition, that stands more substantially in the collective culture and renews its connections with it? To begin to answer the question I would like, first, to talk briefly about my own experience.

I had spent twelve years writing *Icons of Time*, an autobiographical sequence of poems, and when it was complete in 1991 I was anxious to move into a larger much less intimate landscape. Yet it was true that even in writing autobiography I had found it essential to find cultural analogues for my own experience. For example, the collection begins with a quotation from Heraclitus: 'I have searched for myself' (a fragment which lies at the very beginning of Western Classical Culture); and, at a later point, in a sequence about the death of my father, I had found the narrative suddenly descend into the Orpheus myth at the point where the severed head sings and continues to sing on the turbulent water of the tidal current. The Orphic myth, in fact, allowed me to say something about transcendence which could never have been uttered by the authorial 'I'. The language uttered by the mythical person allows one to go where the individual personality cannot speak. In other words, my endeavour to write honest autobiography was, at times, collapsing into myth and collective personae; and it was the promise of that disintegration which, on its completion, I wished to follow. Not for nothing was the closing section named *Moving Out*.

Moving out from self-expression involved moving more sub-stantially into the collective voices of historic culture. I sought to enter more fully into myths, fables, as well as philosophical and artistic lives, not as antiquarian and documentary objects, but as forces which could enter the imagination and be re-collected and re-fashioned there. It was as if these forces were demanding their extension and intensification through this creative encounter. When I came across the following remark by Osip Mandelstam I kept saying to myself : 'yes, that's it; yes, that's it'. I didn't quite understand it but my whole being affirmed the aspiration. Mandelstam wrote:

> One often hears: that is good but it belongs to yesterday. But I say: yesterday has not yet been born. It has not yet really existed. I want Ovid, Pushkin, and Catullus to live once more, and I am not satisfied with the historical Ovid, Pushkin, and Catullus.

Is it that the dead await their resurrection through the imagination of the living? And that the resurrection is not simply a replay but a further transformation? Mandelstam seemed to be asserting just such a radical principle and after the demands of Modernism it seemed utterly compelling. It suggested a different agenda. The poet's task was to consciously pick up and continue the ever unfinished and expectant creation of the past: to rewrite the missing lines of Sappho, to sing again the song of decapitated Orpheus, to compose the lost love songs of Peter Abelard, to relive the deranged breakdown of Nietzsche and the despairing suicide of Virginia Woolf. But more than this it was also to attend to the more hesitant voices, the anguished screams and the desperate silences which marked out lives largely unrecorded and formally unacknowledged. Here the task was to take the microphone to the inarticulate and to turn up the volume; it was also to attempt to fill the alarming gaps with their missing sentences; to make memorable what had gone, for so long, unremembered.

In his book *The Witness of Poetry* Czeslaw Milosz writes:

> Perhaps there is a good craftsman sealed in every poet who dreams about a material already ordered, with ready-made comparisons and metaphors endowed with nearly archetypal affectiveness and, for that reason, universally accepted; what remains then is to work on the language.

This is, no doubt, true. As a writer one can take the elements of any mythical story and soon discover the power that resides there. For example, take the Theseus and Minotaur story. As soon as one locates the bare structural elements of the narrative - the woman with the blue connecting thread, the descent into the labyrinth, the encounter with the beast, the slow ascent, the infallible guide of the thread, the waiting woman - one is pulled into the magnetic field of their power. To engage with them is to engage with archetypal forces sanctioned by a long tradition of story telling. This is unquestionably so, yet in the emerging agenda for my own writing I wanted to include not only repetition but also further elaboration; I wanted the freedom to take the story into new and entirely unexpected patterns of signification. In the case of Theseus and the Minotaur I wanted my less heroic Theseus to reluctantly recognise the darkness of the monster and to make some living pact with it before he was free to return to the surface of the earth and the human relationship which awaited him there. The dark thing had to be acknowledged not, as according to the traditional tale, denied and destroyed through an act of male violence.

But as important as working with (and against) the myths was the desire to make visible the invisible and to make articulate the repressed. For example, it was possible to represent the famous test of Abraham to sacrifice his child, but to tell it from the victim's point of view. In such a move one has merely to push to one side the major character (noble Abraham) and invite the minor character to take the central stage (in the poem it is a psychotherapist's couch). Such a device allows the suppressed voice a dramatic utterance and can alter, at a moment, the seemingly fixed and fatal relationships of the past. In a similar manner, it was possible to take Xanthippe, Socrates' wife, and allow her to speak a piece of her mind with regard to her husband. Xanthippe has been passed down the centuries as a shrew, as the nagging wife, as the female voice of tireless banality and stupidity. Significantly, when in Plato's *The Last Days of Socrates* she comes to visit her husband, she bursts into tears and is coldly reprimanded and dismissed by Socrates, who only desires to explore intellectually the meaning of his imminent death with his disciples. Her brief tearful entrance is judged by the philosopher as silly and excessive and, from then on, she is doomed to be seen as a cipher of female crassness and vulgar feeling. One senses here an act of gross injustice and an alarming failure of feeling at the very birth of philosophy in classical culture. Such a moral catastrophe called for a poem in which Xanthippe could speak, in which her own insight and rage could be expressed and, once again, the invisible rendered visible for all to see, or, at least, an alternative narrative offered for collective contemplation.

I hope these examples have given some idea of the possible scope of retelling. Such writing involves the use of personae, the use of masks; it requires an opening out to the other (who appears to be calling) and then an imaginative identification with that figure and all that it represents in the changing and dialectical story of our long culture. It calls for a very different practice to the dominant one of impressionist mood-writing. Such an approach dissolves our subjective isolation and takes us, as creative agents, into the broader culture. It gives a public face to our despised art; it provides new materials (as ancient as myth) and currents of energy to be tapped and redirected for new purposes.

If, as Czeslaw Milosz prophecies in the quotation which heads this chapter, human kind will increasingly return to the historic past in search of the key to its own enigmatic existence, then the value of such writing is clear. Indeed, such imaginative and transformative reclamation could carry within itself the key to our communal and personal lives. The sequence I have recently finished ends with the quotation from Mandelstam 'I want Ovid, Pushkin and Catullus to live once more' and the following poem:

New Constellations

You do not begin alone; rather, you extend
A narrative. Through the half-open window
The breeze blows in spiked with salt
And distance. Your senses stir until
Your memories rise into new constellations.
Who said there can be no more beauty? That art
Must be minimal or brutal: an ideological aid
Or bare reflection - a mirror laid across
A gallery floor, or some such dull cleverness?
The mind's traffic jams in the maze of the sign,
Ironic civilisation silts and chokes itself.
These words lie dark on the field of the page:
Hard, obdurate grains against the age.

The past, which never truly was, returns again.

(1993)

The Revival of the Mythopoeic: a Study of R S Thomas and Ted Hughes

Since the Second World War the dominant tone of English poetry has been urbane. It is as if, after the seminal work of Eliot, Joyce, Pound and Yeats, the poets moved out to the suburbs choosing for their subject matter the tedious repetitions of domestic life lightened only by the occasional wedding. Like a man meticulously adjusting his tie before his own death, so the poets in English polished their unambitious lines, blind to the vast issues posed by their own moribund civilization. *Not with a bang but with a whimper...*

Two books of poetry, R S Thomas' *H'm* and Ted Hughes' *Crow*, have courageously attempted to move beyond the narrowly fenced backwaters of English poetry. Both books have failings, serious failings, but they do reveal a determination to fashion a new style of poetry, a poetry returning to its dark origins in myth and magic, ritual and chant, while remaining wholly modern in reference. This burrowing back to primeval sources can be felt, at once, in the rhythms of their language. The following lines are taken from the opening poem in *H'm*:

> God looked at space and I appeared,
> Rubbing my eyes at what I saw.
> The earth smoked, no birds sang;
> There were no footprints on the beaches
> Of the hot sea, no creature in it.
> God spoke. I hid myself in the side
> Of the mountain.

These lines are taken from one of the concluding poems in *Crow*:

> Water wanted to live
> It went to the sun it came weeping back
> Water wanted to live
> It went to the trees they burned it came weeping back
> Water wanted to live
> It went to the flowers they crumpled it came weeping back

These short excerpts show the free-ranging style of the poetry, its immediacy, its vastness. The lines from Ted Hughes possess, although the emotion is bitter, the same kind of resonance one finds in the Psalms, in religious litanies, in primitive chants. The words take us beyond their obvious and conventional references into primordial worlds inhabited by warring energies. At the beginning of R S Thomas' poem, we are presented with the creation of man; and at the end, as Adam and Eve move forward 'to meet the Machine', we sense imminent discord and disaster. Both poems work in the manner of myth and yet without any archaism of language, without any academic trappings. The two books represent a powerful attempt to reclaim the great metaphysical issues which, since the Second World War, under the influence of the academic and urbane poets, had seemed beyond the reach of contemporary imagination. Furthermore, the recent poetry of Thomas and Hughes does not evade the burden of industrial experience but attempts through imaginative gestures, to express its nature and influence. R S Thomas writes:

> Knowledge is power;
> The old oracle
> Has not changed. The nucleus
> In the atom awaits
> Our bidding. Come forth,
> We cry, and the dust spreads
> Its carpet. Over the creeds
> And masterpieces our wheels go.

Ted Hughes writes:

> He wanted to sing about her
> He didn't want comparisons with the
>   earth or anything to do with it
> Oversold like detergents
> He did not even want words
> Waving their long tails in public
> With their prostitute's exclamations
>
> He wanted to sing very clear.

Their poetry, struggling to break through the chinks in the dark cavern of Technocracy, throbs with the disturbing vibrations of modern civilization.

It is confirming that both poets, in their different ways, affirm the Romantic conception of the artist, of poets to quote Shelley as 'the hierophants of an unapprehended inspiration: the mirrors of the gigantic shadows which futurity casts upon the present...' In an interview Ted Hughes claimed that, at the present moment, there is:

> a pervasive and deep feeling that civilization has now disappeared completely. If it's still here, it's still here by grace of pure inertia and chance and if the whole thing has essentially vanished one had better have one's spirit invested in something that will not vanish. And this is a shifting of your foundation to completely new Holy Ground, a new divinity, one that won't be under the rubble when the churches collapse.

I wish to question Ted Hughes' new divinity, at least, as it is manifested in *Crow,* but at the moment I am anxious only to draw attention to the ambitious, indeed sublime, conception of the poet. How different it is from the prevailing view about the poet as an ordinary man, with ordinary problems, writing about ordinary things, such as mortgages, cutting the lawn, earning money and dodging work. R S Thomas' conception of the priest-poet is, likewise, magnificent and exhilarating to contemplate:

> My work as a poet has to deal with the presentation of imaginative truth. So that there is no conflict, there's no necessary conflict between these two things at all. As a priest I am committed to the ministry of the word and the ministry of the sacraments. Well, word is metaphor, language is sacrament, the combination is perfectly simple. In presenting the Bible to my congregation I am presenting imaginative interpretation of reality. In presenting the sacrament, administering the sacrament of bread and wine to the congregation, I am again conveying, I'm using a means, a medium of contact with reality... But you should see how these do impinge on each other and there should be no necessary conflict at all. People, no doubt, are worried by the use of the word imagination, because imagination to many people has a fictional connotation, fictional overtones Of course,

I'm using the word imagination in its Coleridgean sense, which is the highest means known to the human psyche of getting into contact with the ultimate reality: imaginative truth is the most immediate way of presenting ultimate reality to a human being.

The comments speak eloquently for themselves. They take us out from isolated pools and stagnant ditches and immerse us, once again, in the deep waters of mythopoeic poetry.

I want now to consider the development of each poet in the light cast by their volumes. First I will look at R S Thomas, then Ted Hughes.

From the beginning, R S Thomas' poetry has been firmly rooted in a landscape, a religion and a community, and it has always embodied conflicting views, desires and interpretations. The conflict, for example, in the early compressed portrait of Iago Prytherch, 'A Peasant', was between a certain admiration for the physical solidity of the man and a certain disquiet over the spiritual vacuity of his mind. In R S Thomas' early work, spiritual beauty and existential fact collide with dramatic energy and fuse with startling effects. In the lines from 'January' describing a wounded fox:

> the crimson seeds
> Of blood burst with a mild explosion,
> Soft as excrement, bold as roses.

how daring and appropriate is the marriage of opposites, the binding of 'burst' with 'mild', of 'excrement' with 'roses'. A relish for contraries, ambiguities, paradoxes darts through the poetry. And, of course, R S Thomas couldn't have found a richer ground for his appetite than Protestant Christianity and 20th century Wales. From the questioning nature of his early poetry, one feels that Thomas' faith is renewed each morning in the manner of an inward argument, a tussle between Belief and Doubt, Death and Resurrection, Spirit and Flesh. And his vision of Wales is, in similar manner, dialectical. It is, as defined in his early poetry, a country torn between the demands of traditional culture and modern civilization, wrenched forward by the gaudy pressures of the present, pulled back by a history "brittle with relics". In his best poems, as in 'A Peasant', 'Welsh Landscape', 'Song at the Year's Turning', 'January', 'Invasion', 'On the Farm', these opposites are yoked lyrically together in a state of high tension.

157

In the later books of R S Thomas, however, one detects what can only be described as poetic exhaustion. In *Not that He Brought Flowers,* for example, many of the poems are rhythmically impotent. Others border heavily on rational exposition. Still others deteriorate into moralistic rant like the following:

> Have a care;
> This wealth is for the few
> And chosen. Those who crowd
> A small window dirty it
> With their breathing, though sublime
> And inexhaustible the view.

More worrying still, a number of poems seemed in danger of parodying their original forerunners. A certain form of expression, once agile and distinctive in movement, seemed to be freezing into a mannerism. The poetry was becoming lifeless because it was predictable. One was beginning to expect 'the gnarled hands on the cheque book', death 'bitter as the soil' and the blackbird's accompaniment 'that promises them love'. Too heavy a reliance on past methods and achievements suggested that the original insights, so boldly projected in the early poetry, were beginning to ossify into habitual responses, gestures without substance, symbols without the flash of vision.

At the same time, in an occasional poem in the later works one became aware of a new energy, audaciously heading out into deep water, an effort - perhaps influenced by Ted Hughes' work - to fashion another poetic style, an effort to open up a new ocean for poetic exploration. In, for example, the poem 'That' all the old preoccupations are cast afresh, given new life and a disturbing universality:

> And endlessly the days go on
> With their business. Lovers make their appearance
> And vanish. The germ finds its way
> From the grass to the snail to the liver to the grass.
> The shadow of the tree falls
> On our acres like a crucifixion,
> With a bird singing in the branches
> What its shrill species has always sung,
> Hammering its notes home
> One by one into our brief flesh.

The poem, in fact, points us directly to the best poems in *H'm*. It has the same freedom of line, the same disturbing breadth of vision, as the following stanzas from 'Repeat':

He touched it. It exploded.
Man was inside with his many
Devices. He turned from him as from his own
Excrement. He could not stomach his grin.
I'll mark you, he thought. He put his finger
On him. The result was poetry:
The lament of Job, Aeschylus,
The grovelling of the theologians.
Man went limping through life, holding
His side.

In *H'm* R S Thomas was seeking to create a radical mythology for the 20th century, a mythology dependent for its vitality on that war between polarities but this time conceived within the mechanical and artificial environment created by the Industrial Revolution. In *H'm* the opposites are seen as transcending the particular contexts of place and community and envisaged as universal energies, God and the Machine, Theocracy and Technocracy, and, as the following quotation shows, Poetry and Production:

The tins marched to the music
Of the conveyor belt. A billion
Mouths opened. Production,
Production, the wheels
Whistled. Among the forests
Of metal the one human
Sound was the lament of
The poets for deciduous language.

The vast conception of human struggle, seen as existing embryonically since the Fall, served to resurrect Thomas' poetry and provided, at the same time, material wholly appropriate to a free-ranging style with which in his middle period he was occasionally experimenting.

One important critical reservation about the achievement of *H'm* has to be registered. I have explicitly praised the free-wheeling lines for through it poetry is able to span disparate experiences,

experiences widely separated by the divisions of space and time, and forge unexpected connections. But, often, in *H'm,* the actual words lack resonance, depth, density. *The poetry lacks physical energy.* It often limps across the page and is far too discursive in manner:

> Mostly it was wars
> With their justifications
> Of the surrender of values
> For which they fought. Between
> Them they laid their plans
> For the next, exempted
> From compact by the machine's
> Exigencies...

> There were people around;
> I would have spoken with them.
> But the situation has got beyond
> Language. Machines were invented
> To cope, but they were also limited
> By our expectations...

The words lack lyrical energy and poetic density. The meanings are explicit, prosaic. The sentences are like those in a treatise or a drab political manifesto: 'But the situation has got beyond language'; 'Machines were invented to cope'; 'the surrender of values'. The words are void of texture. This is true, although to a lesser extent, even in the poems which until this point I have admired. If R S Thomas' recent poems are more ambitious than his earlier ones, they yet lack the verbal music of his first volumes. This is a major loss. And yet, in the same breath, one wishes to point to the positive intentions of *H'm,* the effort to break into new ground, to widen the scope of contemporary poetry, to bring a new burden of universality to poetic themes. R S Thomas has opened the door to a new poetry. It must be hoped that younger poets may now step through.

To leave the matter on this note of newness is, however, somewhat misleading for what R S Thomas is attempting in his recent work is more radical than revolutionary. His poetry is returning us to the roots of the creative imagination. Now as we witness the disintegration of a civilisation based on the laws of reason and matter, a return to the mythopoeic can be understood as a necessary quest for more primitive and more holistic forms of understanding and being.

Ted Hughes' first volume of poetry *The Hawk in the Rain* was published in 1957. The book offered a disparate and uneven collection of poems. Some of the poems were heavy with rhetoric and near-clichés, others were surprisingly delicate and beautifully precise. Some of the poems strutted melodramatically, others were written at a distance, were cool and analytical. And a few of the poems stood out with a strange visionary intensity.

It was very much a *first* book. Ted Hughes was experimenting with different forms and metres, trying the find his own particular voice, his own particular interpretation of experience. Often the experimentation clouds the experience. In the following lines for example:

> But all his efforts to concoct
> The old heroic bang from their money and praise,
> From the parent's pointing fingers and the child's amaze,
> Even from the burning of his wretched bays,
> Have left him wrecked...

One can see that the metrical and rhyming structure has forced the experience into an unconvincing artificial shape. (One wouldn't have expected to find the words 'the child's amaze' in English poetry at any point after Wilfred Owen). At other moments in the volume, one is aware of rather pretentious poems, showing stylistic polish, but no compelling content; exercises in poetic phraseology such as:

> You had to come
> Calling my singularity
> In scorn,
> Imprisonment.
>
> It contained content
> That, now, at liberty
> In your generous embrace,
> At once, in rich Rome,
> Caractacus,
> I mourn.

In a different vein are the diffuse, moralising and banal poems, such as 'The Hag' and 'Law in the Country of the Cats'. Elsewhere, one senses in the poetry the genuine struggle of the poet anxious to create a true form for his own more visionary responses. In the opening stanza of the title poem, the dense accumulation of alliterative words points to a powerful experience desperately seeking order and permanence:

I drown in the drumming ploughland, I drag up
Heel after heel from the swallowing of the earth's mouth,
From clay that clutches my each step to the ankle
With the habit of the dogged grave, but the hawk

Effortlessly at height hands his still eye.

The power of the experience is diffusely felt in these lines but, somehow, not actually embodied. The words clog their meanings. The rhythms are contorted and turn in on themselves. It has an unmistakable poetic quality, but it is not achieved poetry.

Three poems stand out in *The Hawk in the Rain:* 'Wind', 'The Though-Fox', and 'The Horses'. They are too well known to need quotation. It is significant, though, that the three poems are all concerned with Nature, with imposing animals and fierce elements. They are, also, written in free verse held tightly together by alliterative tensions and sharply perceived imagery. These poems held out a promise of a poetry with muscle and sinew, rich with unclouded perceptions and a primitive sympathy for natural energies. The promise was largely fulfilled by the following volumes, *Lupercal* and *Wodwo.*

The most successful poems in these volumes were, once again, preoccupied with the alert world of the wild animal: the pike, the thrush, the otter and the hawk. It was as if the physical power of nature, unchecked by the doubts and burdens of self-consciousness, was being admired for its instinctive poise and unquestioning right to life and action:

... Mozart's brain had it, and the shark's mouth
That hungers down the blood-smell even to a leak of its own
Side and devouring of itself: efficiency which
Strikes too streamlined for any doubt to pluck at it
Or obstruction deflect.

With a man it is otherwise...

With a man it is otherwise because of the power to symbolise, to stand outside of the timeless flux of nature by saying verbs with a past tense and a future as well as a present. The power to symbolise isolates man from nature and renders his own being problematic. The division, then, between man and nature, in Ted Hughes' work, would seem to be sound enough. But Coleridge's suggestion in 'Dejection an Ode' that man sees in nature those qualities he himself places there, casts another light on poems like 'Hawk' and 'Pike'. Are they descriptive nature poems? Or are they poems which select certain animals to symbolise and celebrate *the particular qualities* of violence and manic action? Are the animals more like emblems in a developing mythology than portraits of actual beasts? These questions have disturbing implications. If we decide the poems are descriptive, we can admire their verbal qualities, but, ultimately, must point to their limited range - for what can they tell us about the delights and burdens of human experience? If we decide the poems are essentially symbolic, evoking the nature of human experience, then we must point to their brutality, their failure to recognise the human powers of creativity, tenderness, love and transcendence. The publication of *Crow* suggests we should adopt the latter interpretation.

Before discussing *Crow* I would like to return to the matter of style. I have mentioned already Hughes' liturgical quality. Many lines, like the concluding stanzas from 'Littleblood':

> O littleblood, drumming in a cow's skull
> Dancing with a gnat's feet
> With an elephant's nose with a crocodile's tail.
>
> Grown so wise grown so terrible
> Sucking death's mouldy tits.
>
> Sit on my finger, sing in my ear, O littleblood.

do possess that verbal texture and energy often absent in *H'm*. The lines drive their extraordinary imagery into the marrow of one's bones. It is part of Ted Hughes' genius to be able to convey immense clustering sensations through taut rhythms and original images, although in *Crow*, many of the poems lack economy and controlling restraint. There is an excess of shocking imagery: "Horrors - hairy and slobbery, glossy and raw": "He split his Mammy like a melon/ He was drenched with gore". And sensational words ("sod", "bollocks", "bastard", "jack-boots", "blood-spittle", "guts", etc.) are employed, too frequently, to gain their questionable effects. The work suffers from a crudity, a pounding brutality of language.

163

The poems scream into our brains and, in so doing, destroy the necessary and defining limits of art. In a very short time, as is invariably the case with sensational matter, we cease to respond. *We are unable to respond.* The verbal sensationalism that disfigures many of the poems in *Crow* registers, I believe, a deeper failure, a failure in interpretation, which, returns us to our questions about the intention of Ted Hughes' earlier animal poetry.

If there is doubt about whether 'Hawk' refers to energies and actions beyond the particular species, there can be no doubt about Crow. Crow symbolises the indestructible will to survive. He symbolises energy, endurance, the will to power. 'Examination at the Womb-door' ends with Crow being even more powerful than Death:

> Who is stronger than hope? *Death.*
> Who is stronger than the will? *Death.*
>
> But who is stronger than death?
> > *Me, evidently.*
>
> Pass, Crow.

But we need to ask *how* does Crow survive, in *what sort of world* does he survive, and what does he survive *for*? It is in answering these questions that we confront the failure of *Crow* for, in truth, the book projects a nightmare-universe stripped of meaning and worth. In 'Lineage' we are given the black theology of Crow:

> In the beginning was Scream
> Who begat Blood...
> Who begat God
> Who begat Nothing
> Who begat Never
> Never Never Never
>
> Who begat Crow
>
> Screaming for Blood
> Grubs, crusts
> Anything
>
> Trembling featherless elbows in the nest's filth

Throughout the volume, creation is seen as a disease, "the virus of God", a dark jest in which we are unwittingly embroiled, a jest which only Crow, through a series of evasions and cunning strategies, is able to turn to his own advantage. Birth is seen as a kill, perception as blindness, everything as being grounded in nothing:

> So finally there was nothing.
> It was put inside nothing.
> Nothing was added to it.
> And to prove it didn't exist
> Squashed flat as nothing with nothing.

In such an absurd world, a world shot through with pointlessness, the only aspiration left is the one *to survive at all costs*.

In the interview which I have already quoted, Ted Hughes talked about -

> a complete abolition of everything that's been up to this point and Crow is what manages to drag himself out of it in fairly good morale.

But, as in as much as *Crow* is celebrating *the mere act of survival and making it appear the only possible value,* it must be objected that the poetry denying the powers of love, creativity and reparation, is profoundly nihilistic.

It was Darwin who, in the 19th Century, made current the notion of 'survival of the fittest'. Transferred from Nature (where it may or may not be wholly applicable) to Society it becomes a reductive creed for, on such terms, a gangster or a thug become more worthy than the prophet, the poet, the seminal philosopher and the idealist. Such a transference is also philosophically false for it is blind to that dimension of human existence opened by the power to symbolise: that dimension in which is to be found all those cultural and religious achievements, which distinguish man from nature, to which R S Thomas' poetry is so passionately committed. The failure of *Crow,* unlike *H'm,* consists in its inability to find the essence of man. (I must add here that I do not think this is in any way true of all of Ted Hughes' poetry and of much of the often quite brilliant and affirmative work written after 1970. Perhaps, in retrospect, *Crow* will be interpreted more accurately as a necessary negation, a dark moment of extremity, in the development of his complete work.)

It is always exacting to express clearly a judgement about a poet's achievement. I have looked at R S Thomas, a Welsh poet, and Ted Hughes, an English poet, because they are important contemporary writers who have had the audacity to throw open the doors and windows of a stuffy house. They have made possible a new poetry, broad, free-ranging, essentially mythopoeic. That is a considerable achievement. However, it is important, also, to be aware of the weaknesses that attend new movements so that those who follow may be able to rectify them and so find the formal balance of art. The central weakness in *H'm* is that the language is not generally strong enough to carry its bold content. The major failure of *Crow* is that it is propounding a view of life which deprives man of any purpose and, in the midst of suffering and confusion, of any powers of reparation. It offers us only a black rainbow arched over an abyss where fly violent and unselfconscious creatures. Such a bleak and desperate vision denies us the hope of poetry, conceived as a humanising and liberating force.

Is it possible that we are about to see another revival of the Romantic rebellion against the closed universe of analytical reason? Whatever may be created by such a movement will not be a repetition of archaic images but, rather, a new and largely unforeseeable flowering on ancient wood. Perhaps, it is precisely this sort of development in all the art disciplines, a grafting of the new onto the very old, which will renew our culture and prepare a positive response to what we witness all around us, the steady collapse of rational and materialistic civilisation. Certainly, a study of the recent work of R S Thomas and Ted Hughes brings one to these conclusions.

(1982)

SOURCES AND ACKNOWLEDGEMENTS

The original source of the papers is listed below in order of sequence. The author and publisher would like to thank all those involved in their original publication.

CHAPTER 1: *The Four Fallacies of Modernism* was first published in *Art Monthly*, May 1987.

CHAPTER 2: *The Triumph and Failure of Post-Modernism*. A part of this chapter has previously been published in *Key Concepts: A Guide to Aesthetics, Criticism and the Arts in Education* by Trevor Pateman, Falmer Press, 1991.

CHAPTER 3: *Post-Modernity and the Teaching of the Arts* first appeared as 'Backwards Forward' in *The Times Education Supplement*, April 30th, 1993.

CHAPTER 4: *On the Value and Neglect of the Arts in Education* was first published as Chapter 2 of *Reclamations: Essays on Culture, Mass Culture and the Curriculum*, Heinemann Educational Books, 1979.

CHAPTER 5: *Aesthetic Education: A Manifesto* was first published as Chapter 1 of *The Symbolic Order: a Contemporary Reader on the Arts Debate*, Falmer Press, 1989.

CHAPTER 6: *A Conservationist Aesthetic for Our Schools* was first published as Chapter 9 of *A is for Aesthetic: Essays on Creative and Aesthetic Education*, Falmer Press, 1988.

CHAPTER 7: *Quest for Identity: an Introduction to the Field of Autobiography* first appeared in *The Pelican Guide to English Literature*, edited by Boris Ford, Penguin Books, 1983.

CHAPTER 8: *Autobiography as Individuation: the Strange Case of Edmund Gosse* first appeared as the introduction to Edmund Gosse's *Father and Son*, Penguin English Library, 1983 (revised 1987).

CHAPTER 10: *Uses of Autobiography*. Robert Graham and the author gratefully acknowledge the assistance of a Canadian SSRCH Research Grant No. 410-91-1674 in the preparation of this chapter.

CHAPTER 11: *Born Rural Working Class* has previously appeared in condensed form under the title 'My First Book' in *The Author*, Autumn edition, 1993.

CHAPTER 12: *The Current State of Poetry* has previously been published in *The Use of English*, Autumn Issue, 1993.

CHAPTER 13: *Personae and the Art of Retelling* has previously been published in *Poetry Wales*, Volume 29, Number 2, Autumn 1993.

CHAPTER 14: *The Revival of the Mythopoeic: a Study of R S Thomas and Ted Hughes* has previously been published in *Critical Writings on R S Thomas* edited by Sandra Anstey, Poetry Wales Press, 1982 and 1993.

SELECTIVE BIBLIOGRAPHY

CHAPTER 1

ABBS, P. (ed 1975) *The Black Rainbow,* Heinemann Educational Books.
ABBS, P. (ed 1989) *The Symbolic Order*, Falmer Press.
BERGONZI, B. (ed 1968) *Innovations,* Macmillan.
COMPTON, M. (1974) *Art as Thought,* Arts Council.
EAGLETON, T. (1982) *Literary Theory,* Blackwell.
FULLER, P. (1980) *Beyond the Crisis in Art,* Writers and Readers.
FULLER, P. (1986) *Marches Past,* Chatto and Windus.
PECKHAM, M. (1966) *Man's Rage for Chaos: Biology, Behaviour and the Arts,* Schocken.
POPPER, K. (1957) *The Poverty of Historicism,* Routledge and Kegan Paul.
Y GASSET, O. (1968) *The Dehumanisation of Art,* Princeton University Press.

CHAPTER 2

ABBS, P. (1988) *A is for Aesthetic,* Falmer Press.
COOKE, P. (1990) *Back to the Future,*Unwin Hyman.
JENCKS, C. (1987) *What is Post-Modernism*, Academy Editions.
MORDAUNT CROOK, J. (1987) *The Dilemma of Style,* John Murray.
POPPER, K. (1957), *The Poverty of Historicism,* Routledge and Kegan Paul.

CHAPTER 3

ABBS, P. (1994) *The Educational Imperative: In Defence of Socratic and Aesthetic Learning,* Falmer Press.
OAKESHOTT, M. (1989) *The Voice of Liberal Learning,* Yale University Press.
ROSS, M. (1989) *The Claims of Feeling,* Falmer Press.

CHAPTER 4

DESCARTES, R. *A Discourse on Method,* translated by John Veitch, Everyman's Library, Dent and Sons.
GRENE, M. (1966) *The Knower and the Known,* London, Faber and Faber.
LANGER, S. (1957) *Philosophy in a New Key,* Harvard University Press.

169

LOCKE, J. *An Essay Concerning Human Understanding,* edited by Raymond Wilburn, Everyman's Library, Dent and Sons.

MILL, J.S. *Autobiography and Literary Essays,* edited by John Robson and Jack Stillinger, University of Toronto Press.

MUMFORD, L. (1971) *The Myth of the Machine,* Secker and Warburg.

PASCAL, B. *Pascal's Pensées,* Everyman's Library, Dent and Sons.

PLATO, *The Republic,* translated by B Jowett, Oxford University Press, 1871.

CHAPTER 5

BEST, D. (1985) *Feeling and Reason in the Arts,* George Allen and Unwin.

BROOK, P. (1988) *The Shifting Point,* Methuen.

GOMBRICH, E. (1984) *Tributes,* Phaidon.

PATER, W. (1873) *The Renaissance,* Macmillan.

ROBINSON, K. (1988) *The Arts and the National Curriculum,* National Association for Education through the Arts, UK, Occasional Paper Vol.3.

WAY, B. (1967) *Development through Drama,* Longman.

WOOLF, V. (1976) 'Letter to a Poet' in *Collected Essays,* Volume 2, Harcourt Brace.

CHAPTER 6

ADSHEAD, J. (1981) *The Study of Dance,* Dance Books.

CARLYLE-HAYNES, A. (1987) 'Changing Perspectives in Dance Education' in Abbs, P. (ed) *Living Powers: the Arts in Education,* Falmer Press.

FRAMPTON, K. (1983) 'Towards a critical regionalism. Six points for an architecture of resistance' in *Post-Modern Culture,* Pluto Press.

FULLER, P. (1986) *Images of God,* Chatto and Windus.

GARDNER, H. (1984) *Frames of Mind: the Theory of Multiple Intelligence,* Heinemann.

GOMBRICH, E. *Tributes: Interpretations of our Cultural History,* Phaidon.

HABERMAS, J. (1983) 'Modernity - an Incomplete Project' in *Post-Modern Culture,* Pluto Press.

KANT, I. *The Critique of Judgement* translated by James Meredith, Oxford University Press.

MIDGLEY, M. (1970) *Beast and Man,* Harvester Press.

MORDAUNT CROOK, J. (1987) *The Dilemma of Style,* John Murray.

POPPER, K. (1957) *The Poverty of Historicism,* Routledge and Kegan Paul.

READ, H. (1944) *Paul Nash,* Penguin Books.

ROBERTSON, S. (1982) *Rosegarden and Labyrinth: A Study in Art Education,* Gryphon Press.

STEERS, J. (1983) *The Journal of Art and Design Education.*

TAYLOR, R. (1986) *Education for Art*, Longmans.
TAYLOR, R. (1992) *The Visual Arts in Education*, Falmer Press.

CHAPTER 7

MUIR, E. (1980) *An Autobiography*, The Hogarth Press.
OLNEY, J. (1972) *Metaphors of Self: the Meaning of Autobiography*, Princeton University Press.
PASCAL, R. (1960) *Design and Truth in Autobiography*, Routledge and Kegan Paul.
RAINE, K. (1991) *Autobiographical Trilogy*, Skoob Books.
READ, H. (1963) *The Contrary Experience*, Secker and Warburg.
SPENGEMANN, W. (1980) *The Forms of Autobiography*, Yale University Press.
WETHERED, H.N. (1956) *The Curious Art of Autobiography*, Johnson.
WOOLF, V. (1976) 'A Sketch of the Past' in *Moments of Being: Unpublished Autobiographical Writing*, Chatto and Windus.

CHAPTER 8

ABBS, P. (1974) *Autobiography in Education*, Heinemann Educational Books.
BRUGMAN, L. (1960) *Correspondence of André Gide and Edmund Gosse*, Owen.
BUCKLEY, J. (1984) *The Turning Key*, Harvard University Press.
CHARTERIS, E. (1931) *The Life and Letters of Sir Edmund Gosse*, Heinemann.
FLEISHMAN, A. (1983) *Figures and Autobiography*, University of California Press.
GRYLLS, D. (1978) *Guardians and Angels*, Faber and Faber.
LANDOW, G. (1979) *Approaches to Victorian Autobiography*, Ohio University Press.
MORRIS, J. (1966) *Versions of the Self*, Basic Books.
NICHOLSON, H. (1927) *The Development of English Biography*, Hogarth Press.
OLNEY, J. (1972) *Metaphors of Self*, Princeton University Press.
OLNEY, J. (1980) *Autobiography: Essays Theoretical and Critical*, Princeton University Press.
PASCAL, R. (1960) *Design and Truth in Autobiography*, Routledge and Kegan Paul.
PATEMAN, T. (1986) *Autobiography and Education*, University of Sussex, Occasional Paper 13.
PETERSON, L. (1986) *Victorian Autobiography: the Tradition of Self Interpretation*, Yale University Press.
SHUMAKER, W. (1954) *English Autobiography*, University of California Press.
STRACHEY, L. (1981) *Eminent Victorians*, Penguin.
STURROCK, J. (1993) *The Language of Autobiography*, Cambridge University Press.

THWAITE, A. (1984) *Edmund Gosse; A Literary Landscape*, Secker and Warburg.

WEINTRAUB, K. (1978) *The Value of the Individual: Self and Circumstance in Autobiography*, University of Chicago.

WOOLF, V. (1967) *Collected Essays*, Vol.IV, Hogarth Press.

CHAPTER 9

ABBS, P. (1991) *Icons of Time*, Gryphon Press.

BARTLETT, F.C. (1968) *Remembering: A Study in Experimental and Social Psychology*, Cambridge University Press.

READ, H. (1963) *The Contrary Experience*, Secker and Warburg.

UPDIKE, J. (1989) *Self-Consciousness*, André Deutsch.

WOOLF, V. (1976) 'A Sketch of the Past' in *Moments of Being: Unpublished Autobiographical Writing*, Chatto and Windus.

CHAPTER 10

ABBS, P. (1973) *Autobiography in Education*, Heinemann Educational Books.

ABBS, P. (1988) *A is for Aesthetic*, Falmer Press.

GRAHAM, R. (1992) *Reading and Writing the Self*, New York, Teachers College Press.

JUNG, C. (1963) *Memories, Dreams, Reflections*, Fontana.

CHAPTER 12

ALVAREZ, A. (1962) *The New Poetry*, Penguin.

FEIRSTEIN, F. (1989) *Essays on the New Narrative and the New Formalism*, Story Line Press.

HULSE, M., KENNEDY, D., MORLEY, D. (1993) *The New Poetry*, Bloodaxe.

McDOWELL, R. (1991) *Poetry after Modernism*, Story Line Press.

CHAPTER 13

ABBS, P. (1991) *Icons of Time*, Gryphon Press.

ABBS, P. (1994) *Personae and Other Selected Poems*, Skoob Books.

LAWRENCE, D.H. (1970) 'Preface to the American Edition of New Poems' in *Selected Essays*, Penguin.

MANDELSTAM, O. (1991) *The Collected Critical Prose and Letters*, edited by Jane Harris, Collins Harvill.

MILOSZ, C. (1983) *The Witness of Poetry*, Harvard University Press.

HUGHES, T. (1957) *The Hawk in the Rain,* Faber and Faber.
HUGHES, T. (1961) *Lupercal,* Faber and Faber.
HUGHES, T. (1970) *Crow,* Faber and Faber.
THOMAS, R.S. (1955) *Song at the Year's Turning,* Hart Davis.
THOMAS, R.S. (1968) *Not That He Brought Flowers,* Hart Davis.
THOMAS, R.S. (1972) *H'm,* Macmillan.

further titles from

SKOOB BOOKS PUBLISHING

AUTOBIOGRAPHIES
Kathleen Raine

Opening with a magical evocation of childhood in a remote Northumbrian hamlet during the First World War, *Autobiographies* is an illuminating attempt to chart the inner life of one of the most eminent poets of our time.

'Beautifully written... A life of seeking, suffering, in love with nature and her eternal world, the spiral of the seasons... and above all of hard creative work all of which bears the stamp of her remarkable genius... story of a beautiful and unique spirit.'   *Chapman*

ISBN 1 871438 41 1   Pbk   £12.99

STRING OF BEGINNINGS
Michael Hamburger
Intermittent Memoirs 1924-1954

'His admirably hardheaded and wholehearted commitment to humanity breathes from cover to cover of this candid, seriously humorous recapitulation from a life dedicated to practical and intellectual virtue.'   *Jewish Chronicle*
'Fine and memorable'   *Poetry Review*

ISBN 1 871438 66 7   Pbk   £10.99

COLLECTED JOURNALS 1936-42
David Gascoyne

These journals illuminate and complement his poetry and reaffirm David Gascoyne as a major poetic voice of the twentieth century.

'...Gascoyne has long seemed an outsider in the history of modern English poetry and these brilliant and fascinating Journals, in which the keeping of a diary is raised to the condition of literature, explain why.'   *Stand*

ISBN 1 871438 50 0   Pbk   £10.99

AVAILABLE FROM ALL GOOD BOOKSHOPS
OR ORDER FROM SKOOB TWO WITH A CREDIT CARD, TEL 0171 405 0030 DELIVERY POST FREE IN UK.
A DISCOUNT OF 20% IS AVAILABLE WHEN YOU ORDER TWO BOOKS OR MORE, DIRECT FROM SKOOB.

SKOOB *Pacifica*

Contemporary writings of the Pacific Rim and South Asia

Skoob Pacifica is a new series which brings to a wider reading public the best in contemporary fiction, poetry, drama and criticism from the countries of the Pacific Rim. The flagship of the series, the Skoob Pacifica Anthology, presents selections from many of our featured authors alongside those of more established names.

SKOOB PACIFICA ANTHOLOGY No.1
S.E.Asia Writes Back!
I.K.Ong & C.Y.Loh (editors)

An eclectic blend of prose, poetry, drama and reportage which creates a vibrant picture of the post-colonial world. Featured writers include Vikram Seth, Yukio Mishima and Wole Soyinka, with short stories by Yasunari Kawabata and Derek Walcott.

ISBN 1 871438 19 5   432pp   £5.99

SKOOB PACIFICA ANTHOLOGY No.2
The Pen is Mightier Than The Sword

This second anthology focuses on exciting and challenging writing from Malaysia and Singapore in the 1990s. Also featured are pieces by Han Suyin, Toni Morrison and V.S. Naipaul.

ISBN 1 871438 54 3   412pp   £6.99

SKOOB PACIFICA ANTHOLOGY No.3
Exiled in Paradise

In this third volume, the scope of the series is extended to include South Asia, an important area of new writing. It also contains poetry from the Philippines, and includes work from Naguib Mahfouz, Nadine Gordimer and Shirley Geok-lin Lim.

ISBN 1 871438 59 4   432pp   £6.99   Available Spring 1996

---

further titles from
SKOOB BOOKS PUBLISHING

Gothic reading for winter evenings

THE QUEEN'S DIADEM
C.J.L. Almqvist
Translated by Yvonne L. Sandstroem

With a Foreword by George C. Schoolfield and an essay by Marilyn J. Blackwell

A convicted poisoner, Almqvist (1793-1866) ranks in Scandinavian literature with Ibsen, Kierkegaard and Strindberg. His extraordinary gothic novel *The Queen's Diadem* is here translated into English for the first time.

ISBN 1 871438 21 7   Pbk   £8.99   (not U.S.A)

Two of the original gothic novels from the Northanger Abbey septet

THE MIDNIGHT BELL
Francis Lathom

A story of greed and jealousy, of uncontrollable passions and the disasters they bring.
'My father is now reading *The Midnight Bell*, which he has got from the library, and mother sitting by the fire.'

Jane Austen's letter to Cassandra, 24 October 1798

ISBN 1 871438 30 6   Pbk   £5.95 $10.95

THE NECROMANCER
Peter Teuthold

A detective novel first published in 1794, *The Necromancer* is an exploration of fear and the power of secrecy. This is traditional gothic with dark Germanic settings, charnel-houses and chains.

ISBN 1 871438 20 9   Pbk   £4.95 $8.95

CHAPBOOKS OF THE EIGHTEENTH CENTURY
Ed. John Ashton

A fascinating window onto the heroes and legends, folklore and superstitions of the period. This collection contains over one hundred chapbooks with facsimiles of the original woodcut illustrations.

ISBN 1 871438 26 8   Pbk   £9.95 $19.95

AVAILABLE FROM ALL GOOD BOOKSHOPS
OR ORDER FROM SKOOB TWO WITH A CREDIT CARD, TEL 0171 405 0030 DELIVERY POST FREE IN U.K.
A DISCOUNT OF 20% IS AVAILABLE WHEN YOU ORDER TWO BOOKS OR MORE, DIRECT FROM SKOOB.